Plays by the author

Laura   (with Vera Caspary)

Merry Go Round   (with Albert Maltz)
Peace on Earth

Stevedore   (with Paul Peters)
Parade

Life and Death of An American

And People All Around

Novels:

The Two Worlds of Johnny Truro
The Promising Young Men
The Housewarming
The Identity of Dr. Frazier

AND PEOPLE ALL AROUND

AND
PEOPLE
ALL AROUND

GEORGE SKLAR

 Random House . New York

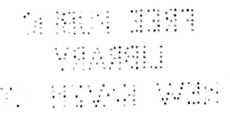

Library of Congress Catalog Card Number: 67–22670

Manufactured in the United States of America
by The Book Press Incorporated, Brattleboro, Vermont

*To Miriam, Judy, Dan, and Zach
with a bow to the American Playwrights Theatre*

Although there are episodes in this play which may suggest actual happenings of the summer of '64, they are not
meant to portray those happenings or the people who were
involved in them. The characters, the plot, the actions are
fictional, and no resemblance to persons, living or dead, is
intended. The town of Leucadia does not, in fact, exist.
It is, rather, an imagined composite of many towns.

Act One

PROLOGUE

The curtain rises on a virtually dark stage. We hear the wail of a siren, which rises, wanes, and rises again. Vaguely discernible are running figures. The movement is chaotic— as random, compulsive and directionless as that of a demonstration being dispersed, which, we soon realize, is precisely what is happening. A few overhead spots go on, throwing distinct shafts of light yet leaving a hazy overall spill which gives the illusion of dust rising.

Figures run pell-mell, wheel, dodge, stumble, fall and pick themselves up again. The pursuers are distinguished from those pursued by their white helmets and swinging police clubs. The total effect is one of panic; the air vibrates with violence, with grunts and groans and sudden cries, with the blurred sound of bullhorns, with the barking of police dogs, one of which bounds across stage, the figures darting to either side to avoid it.

A Negro staggers into one of the spotlights, covering his head with his hands. The completely limp figure of another Negro is dragged by the legs down a short flight of stairs, his head jouncing on the steps.

A spotlight picks out a white girl, her face streaming with blood. She is sobbing. Another spot comes up on three Negro girls kneeling in prayer.

Several shots are heard. There is a sudden silence as all turn to see a Negro on the stairs, clutching at his stomach, a look of agony on his face. He slumps and falls down the stairs. The siren rises as the lights dim, then fades into silence.

Angled spots come up on the CHORUS OF COMMENTATORS. *It is comprised of men and women, Negro and white, who stand facing the audience in a tight, triangular formation. The resonant bong of a clock striking six is heard.*

FIRST MAN   When the clock from the courthouse sounded the end of day, a seemly quiet had returned to Constitution Square.

FIRST WOMAN   A serenity belying the discord, the roiled passions and bitterness, lay over the town.

SECOND WOMAN   Twilight falls softly on the streets of Leucadia.

SECOND MAN   The sun sinking over the pines on Honey Hill leaves a wash of muted pinks, orange and gold.

THIRD WOMAN   The mingled scents of sweet blossoming dogwood, of Cherokee roses, azaleas and jasmine—

FIRST WOMAN   Suffuse the senses.

THIRD MAN   And a stranger, arriving for the first time in this lovely valley known as the Soul of the Southland—

FIRST MAN   Would never suspect.

SECOND MAN   That here.

FIRST WOMAN   On Constitution Square.

THIRD MAN   Blood ran.

FIRST MAN   And death spoke from the barrel of a .38 Police Positive.

SECOND WOMAN   That the beds in Leucadia are inadequate to accommodate the wounded.

THIRD MAN   And the jails of Leucadia, Jubel, Jefferson and Chattahoochie unable to contain—

FIRST WOMAN   The one thousand eight hundred and thirty arrested in the five preceding days of that fateful summer of 1964.
    (*The* CHORUS *moves forward a few steps*)

THIRD WOMAN   They came to register, they said.

SECOND MAN   To redeem a promissory note signed one hundred years ago, as one of them put it.

FIRST MAN   To obstruct traffic and disturb the peace, said the Sheriff.

FIRST WOMAN (*With quickening tempo*)   Leucadia is an expanding city.

SECOND WOMAN   With a fast-growing population.

FIRST MAN   It boasts of—

THIRD WOMAN   Its schools and playgrounds.

FIRST WOMAN   A balanced budget and low crime rate.

THIRD MAN   It offers an open shop and ample labor—

FIRST MAN   To supply its new textile and plane plants.

SECOND MAN Its sour-mash distillery and lumber mill.

FIRST WOMAN An open town.

FIRST MAN (*Stepping out of formation; the others follow to make a loose grouping*) Yessir, it's *wide* open, boys.

SECOND MAN Walk in any corner drug- or cigar store and put two bucks on Sunshine in the fourth.

THIRD MAN Or pick your winning number, man.

FIRST MAN Or if you want yourself a fix—

THIRD MAN Or tail.

SECOND MAN Why you wander around to—

FIRST MAN Tootsie's.

SECOND MAN Or Mable's.

THIRD MAN Or the Redhead's.

FIRST WOMAN (*Stepping forward*) Come on up, boys. We can give it to you any way you like—black and tan, high yaller or white, French style, Singapore, or Birmingham style.

FIRST MAN Shake it, sister! Shake that thing!
(FIRST WOMAN *does a few bumps and grinds. Then the* CHORUS *returns into its tight formation*)

SECOND WOMAN Yessir, it's a very friendly town.

THIRD WOMAN A God-fearing town, with eighteen churches.

6

FIRST WOMAN   Visitors are invited to join in worship.

FIRST MAN   They are also invited to meetings of the Kiwanis, Rotary, Lions, and Chamber of Commerce.

SECOND MAN   And to certain meetings of the Supreme Order of White Redeemers.

THIRD MAN   The White Redeemers, you know, is a secret order.

FIRST MAN   It has secret rites, obligations, and activities.

SECOND MAN   And in the dark of night when owls hoot and hyenas call and strange spirits roam the hills—

FIRST MAN   The bond is pledged.

THIRD MAN   The deed is done. (*A hair-rising cry is heard. The* CHORUS *wheels toward it*) And, rest assured, all will continue to be as it has been.
(*The* CHORUS *returns to original position*)

FIRST MAN   This is Leucadia.

SECOND MAN   A good place—if you know your place.

FIRST WOMAN   But let us be fair.

SECOND WOMAN   This town is no better or worse than any other. It has its good and bad.

THIRD MAN   And the majority do not approve of what happens in the hills.

THIRD WOMAN   Nor are they happy about the events in Constitution Square.

FIRST MAN Sitting at home tonight, anxious and disturbed, they hope for an end to what has already gone too far.

FIRST WOMAN For death is not a casual thing—as the Negroes mourning at the First Baptist Church so very well know.

SECOND WOMAN On Sycamore Street a young man, visiting his fiancée who has just returned from a shopping trip to Atlanta, waits for her to try on a newly bought dress. (*Lights dim on the* CHORUS *and come up on the other side of the stage. The young man,* DON TINDALL, *twenty-eight, tall, lean, with attractive, rugged features, is seated at a small upright piano. He picks out a few aimless, moody chords; then, as if suddenly impatient, hits a jangle of discord, and swivels around on the piano bench*)

DON (*Calling tentatively*) Gwen . . .

GWEN (*Offstage*) Be right with you, darling. Close your eyes and don't open them till I say "now." Hear? (*He does so.* GWEN GRAYSON, *twenty-two, blond, a suggestion of languor in her well-proportioned figure, walks onstage from the darkness. A spot hits her as she draws herself up in a regal pose before* DON. *She is dressed in a full-length, white lace wedding gown. Perched on her head is a becoming white circlet and, draped from it, a long veil. Her face is flushed, her full lips provocatively parted*) Now. (DON *opens his eyes, looks at her in silence*) I know I shouldn't be showing you the gown before the wedding, but I'm so excited I couldn't resist. Are you angry with me?

DON No.

GWEN But you're not saying anything. Don't you like it?

DON It's—pretty.

GWEN I had a suspicion you wouldn't. There was another one—a little simpler. Perhaps I should have chosen it.

DON There's nothing wrong with your choice.

GWEN Then what?

DON Nothing. It's just that—

GWEN (*Sitting down on the bench beside him*) Don . . .

DON What?

GWEN (*Looking up at him*) Kiss me? (*He does so, perfunctorily*) You're displeased with me. I kept you waiting and I—

DON It's not you.

GWEN But you're so moody. Not like yourself. Something's bothering you. What?

DON I don't know. I've been out of sorts all day. The whole idea, I suppose.

GWEN Of what? The wedding? I don't understand.

DON I don't understand myself. It's everything. Everything that's going on in this town.

9

GWEN   We're all upset by what's happening. Who wouldn't be? You can get downright morbid if you think about it. Let's not. Not now.

DON (*Getting up*)   I can't think of anything else.

GWEN   That's not very flattering—considering that our wedding's only a week away.

DON   These things *are* happening, Gwen. I *am* concerned.

GWEN (*Rising from the bench*)   You're always concerned about other people—and I love you for it. But right now I wish you'd act like a bridegroom. I fall asleep and wake up seeing us walk down that aisle.

DON   I wish you'd forget the big wedding, Gwen. Why can't we go to a justice of the peace and avoid all the fuss?

GWEN   You agreed to a church wedding.

DON   Considering what's going on, I don't think a big ceremony and lavish banquet at the country club are either timely or appropriate.

GWEN   I don't like what's going on. But what's it got to do with you and me?

DON   A man was killed today, Gwen.

GWEN   *We* weren't out there shooting guns. *We're* not beating nigras . . . Oh, dear. Why'd it have to happen now?
      (*She sits on the bench again*)

DON   Sooner or later it was bound to.

GWEN   I wish Mama hadn't sent out the invitations. Because we could postpone it a few weeks.

DON   The violence may be over in a few weeks, but the feeling won't be.

GWEN   The timing *was* unfortunate.

DON   The timing for any murder is unfortunate.

GWEN   Mama had no way of knowing. She invited two hundred guests. We can't *un*invite them. We can't offend people.

DON   We can't offend. But we can maim and kill.

GWEN (*Angrily*)   That's unfair! You have no right to—

DON (*Sitting down beside her*)   It *was* uncalled for and I apologize.

GWEN   You make it sound as if I had something to do with it, when I think it's perfectly awful. Why don't you put the blame where it belongs! On those outsiders who came in and stirred things up. We never had any trouble with our nigras.

DON   Your brother-in-law Steve and his fellow Redeemers have seen to that.

GWEN   Oh, that Steve! Not because of the Redeemers. But because we understand our nigras and they understand us. And because they've been happy.

DON   Happy people don't go into the street and risk their lives, Gwen.

GWEN   Do you approve of their going out and parading in the street? You seem to be more concerned about them than you are about me. I don't believe you care what *I* want or feel. I don't believe you love me or want to get married. You've been at me all evening. You want out. Admit it.

DON   I want out of a big wedding at this particular time, yes.

GWEN   You want out entirely. Don't you think I know! You think I'm going to beg you? Why don't you go down to that Cofo Center and find yourself one of those nice nigger girls you're so upset about. Why don't you marry one of them?

DON   When you calm down, perhaps we can talk sensibly.

GWEN   I don't want to talk! I don't want to see you! (DON *stands uncertain*) Why don't you go!

DON (*Shrugs, starts to go, and pauses*)   Now, look, Gwen.

GWEN   Go, damn you!
        (DON *turns and walks on. The lights dim. We hear a recording of "Downtown." A spot picks up* DON, *who sits on a stool facing the audience*)

DON   On the way home I stopped at the Green Lantern. I sat at the bar trying to make sense out of what had happened. There'd been no thought of breaking with Gwen. But she was right—consciously or unconsciously—I'd provoked it. And I felt guilty—and relieved. Was I in love with her? I don't know. She was pretty, we found meaningless things to chatter about, we played tennis, did everything but go to bed together. She always drew the line, teasing me with promises of how wonderful it would be after we got married. Was that why I was marrying her? I wrote her a letter saying it was better over. Strange the way those five days seemed to affect things. It was as if I'd been myopic and suddenly put on glasses and it was all different. The town, the people, Gwen, my awareness that the "happy nigra" wasn't at all happy. (*He rises*) In the mail that day there was an invitation to a party honoring the students who'd come down to work for civil rights. I didn't plan to go. I wasn't sure that I approved of their coming down, and I knew I didn't want to get involved. But it came from Lloyd Lewis, a Negro I'd played with as a kid—and it bothered me. Lloyd and I were best friends until long after we knew colored and white couldn't be best friends.

VOICE OF DON'S FATHER (*Offstage*)   It isn't that we've got anything against Lloyd, son. He's a good boy. But he's black and you're white and that's the way things are.

DON   But I like him. I don't have any other friends.

VOICE OF DON'S FATHER   You'll find 'em—among your own.

DON   Yes, Dad . . . I continued to see Lloyd. We'd meet in Beauregard Woods to finish a cabin we were putting together.

VOICE OF YOUNG LLOYD   (*Offstage*)   Know something, Don? I think birds must be smarter than people.

DON   Because they can fly?

VOICE OF YOUNG LLOYD   Be fun to fly. But they've got so much sense. When it gets cold they take off for where it's warm, two thousand, three thousand miles maybe. And when it warms up they know just how to make their way back. To the exact spot, like that phoebe there.

DON   Dad can't even find his way back from Jubel. He always takes the wrong turn . . . I didn't see Lloyd again till a few years ago when my folks were killed in an air crash. Ironically, it was in answer to a condolence letter that I invited him up to the house. He'd been to Howard University, was teaching at the Negro high school, and we found much to talk about. The old liking was there. But that was that—until the note. (*He walks to a table*) It was on my mind at the office the next day. I was working on plans for a factory I'd designed for Paper Products, Inc.
    (FRANK SIMS, *a man in his mid-thirties, steps into the lighted area.* DON *is looking at blueprints on the table*)

FRANK   Pretty well along, I see. And damn attractive.

DON   Thanks.

FRANK   I only hope it doesn't turn out to be a waste motion.

DON (*Looking up*)   Why? Is Paper Products having second thoughts about locating in Leucadia?

FRANK   There's a lot of pressure on them not to.

DON   I wouldn't blame them if they didn't. It certainly won't help public relations.

FRANK   Not nationally, no.

DON (*Pulling the note out of his pocket*)   Speaking about public relations, what do you feel about my going to this?

FRANK (*Glancing at it*)   Why? Are you planning to?

DON   Not really. But I'm toying with the idea. What do you think?

FRANK   Hell, that's between you and your conscience . . . You really want my advice? Put five twenty-dollar bills in an envelope and mail it.
(*He walks offstage*)

DON   That didn't really answer my problem. Because I was still troubled. But it did go a long way toward salving my conscience.
(*Light dims. We hear the sound of a guitar, and a voice singing "Go Tell It on the Mountain." Light comes up on* LLOYD LEWIS, *his foot on a chair as he plays and sings. Around him is a mixed group, some standing, some sitting on the floor. He is an attractive Negro in his late twenties. There is an intensity in his lean features*)

LLOYD (*Singing*)
Go tell it on the mountain
Over the hill and everywhere,
Go tell it on the mountain
To let my people go.

Who's that yonder, dressed in white?
Let my people go.
Must be the children of the Israelites,
Let my people go.

Go tell it on the mountain
Over the hill and everywhere,
Go tell it on the mountain

To let my people go.

(*As he finishes the song he notices* DON, *who has come into periphery of the lighted area during the song. He hands the guitar to a girl. Others go on humming the song.* LLOYD *comes around to welcome* DON. *There is a warmth in their greeting. The light dims on the rest of the party as they talk*)

LLOYD   Don! I'm glad you came. I was hoping you would.

DON   But you weren't sure.

LLOYD   Sure enough to make a bet on it. Which I intend to collect.

DON   You have more faith in me than I have. I circled around for half an hour trying to get up the guts. And when I did, I parked four blocks away.

LLOYD   They're probably taking license numbers, so it's just as well. How about a drink? It's punch.

DON   Fine.
(LLOYD *turns to the table and pours a drink from a pitcher into a paper cup*)

LLOYD   I'm sorry I put you on the spot, but things are getting pretty rough and we need help, Don.

DON   I wish you'd asked for it before you started all this. Because from where I sit, this isn't the—

LLOYD   It's the only way that'll get results. We've tried everything else.

DON (*Shrugging*)   I don't know what you think *I* can do.

16

LLOYD You went to school with the Sheriff . . .

DON Grammar school.

LLOYD But you know him.

DON Or thought I did—until he started cracking skulls.

LLOYD I wonder what'd happen if you got together a few friends and tried talking to him.

DON On this issue? You might as well talk to Supreme Wizard Dorrance R. Medford.

LLOYD Paper Products cancelled its contract, I'm told.

DON This morning.

LLOYD Doesn't he understand the implications for the town—just in dollars and cents?

DON Sure he understands. But he's fighting to preserve a way of life. And he can be damn ruthless when it's threatened.

LLOYD That's for sure. (*He sighs*) Well, I invited you to a party.

DON (*Raising the cup to toast*) Here's to it.

LLOYD (*Touching his cup to* DON's) It's good to see you— even under these circumstances. (*They sip*) I want you to meet some of the gang.
      (*The lights spread to include* BETTY *and* LOU MAR-CUS, *who are seated on a step nearby.* LOU *is an amiable-looking man in his mid-twenties;* BETTY *is*

small, tidy, attractive. With them is JEAN PORTUGAL, *twenty-three, vital, theatric-looking*)

LLOYD   Don Tindall . . . Betty and Lou Marcus, Jean Portugal . . . The Marcuses are from Detroit and started the Center here. Jean's one of our summer volunteers from New York.

DON   Don't get up. Please.

LOU   For an authentic Leucadian who comes to a COFO party, I certainly will. (*He bows with mock ceremony and extends his hand*) Welcome.
(DON *shakes hands with him*)

LLOYD   Two bits, please.

LOU (*Taking a coin out of his pocket*)   That's one bet I don't mind losing. It's hard getting hold of you people. We can't phone because phones are tapped; can't visit because we're tailed. So we send little love notes. The only answers have been two anonymous letters with five twenty-dollar bills. (DON *chuckles*) What's so funny? Did you send one?

DON   I plead guilty. And I can guess the other.

LOU   I was beginning to think you were a myth. You're the first one who doesn't seem to feel we're highly contagious.

BETTY   As a matter of fact, we are.

LOU   What're you doing? Scaring off the only one who's had the guts to show.

DON   Not that I'm sure I should have, or that what you're doing is right.

18

JEAN What're we doing?

DON Reviving the Civil War, according to some.

LLOYD Was it ever over?

DON You think the violence is going to help?

BETTY You arrange for it to stop and we'll all say hallelujah.

DON If you stop your marches, maybe it will.

LOU What you mean is that if we stop our marches, demonstrations, and any and all attempts to get the Negroes of this county registered, then everything'll be peachy and dandy.

DON What I mean is that there are other ways.

LLOYD Such as taking tests with questions like "How many bubbles in a bar of soap?"

DON I'm just as opposed to those tests as you are, Lloyd. All I'm saying is that you're playing right into the hands of the Redeemers. Those marches are perfect provocation to violence.

LOU We're not the ones who're swinging clubs.

DON Neither would they if you weren't here.

LOU You mean you think the Southerners ought to handle it . . . You have.

DON And we've been slow about it, I know.

19

LLOYD   A hundred years slow.

DON   The question is: can you force things?

LOU   The question is: can you let things go on the way they are?

BETTY   As a Southerner, what have *you* done, Mr. Tindall —aside from sending twenty-dollar bills?

DON   Not much, I admit.

JEAN   He's here.

DON   Drinking punch and wondering why.

JEAN   Are we that uncongenial?

DON (*His eyes meeting hers*)   No . . .

JEAN   Not much conviction in that. We're not ogres, we don't wear horns. Really.

DON (*Smiling*)   You don't have to persuade me. Although I'm not so sure about my fellow townsmen.

LLOYD (*Sitting on the bench beside him*)   What would your townsmen think if they found out we were planning a boycott of every white store in the county?

DON   The businessmen wouldn't like it.

LLOYD   Fine. Then maybe they'll do something.

LOU (*Sitting on the other side of* DON)   Maybe they'd be interested if someone tipped them off about it.

DON   And that someone is me?

LLOYD   You or your partner.

DON   Look, don't box me in. Now I know why I circled
around for half an hour!
(*Gets up and walks a few steps*)

LLOYD   Well, if you don't think they'd be concerned—

DON (*Turning*)   Where'd I get this information?

LOU   You heard a rumor and were disturbed—as they will
be. Maybe enough to get the Mayor to call off this war.

DON   The Mayor wants to be next Governor of the state.

LOU   He won't be if the town goes bankrupt. Look, why
don't you give it a try?

BETTY   Stop pushing the man, Lou. You're making him
very uncomfortable.

LOU   All right, no pushing. My wife has spoken—and I al-
ways listen to my wife. Hey, that punch bowl needs filling.
(*He picks it up.* BETTY, LOU, *and* LLOYD *exit, leaving*
DON *with* JEAN)

DON (*After a pause*)   Well?

JEAN   Well, what?

DON   Wasn't that your cue to go to work on me?

JEAN   You've been reading too many James Bonds.

DON Not that he gives a guy much choice.

JEAN He knows what he's after.

DON And you?

JEAN I'm here.

DON That's what you said about me. But you came all the way from New York. Why? Why should a pretty girl like you—

JEAN Does "pretty" mean I don't have brains or convictions?

DON No, of course not.

JEAN Then what kind of a crack was that?

DON It was my stupid way of saying I thought you were attractive. But I still don't understand why you—

JEAN I almost didn't. I was working on a program for a modern dance group.

DON Ha! I knew there was something theatrical about you. You carry yourself like a dancer.

JEAN And just how do dancers carry themselves?

DON I seem to be saying all the wrong things. I met a couple of dancers at Yale. They had a certain kind of bearing. A sort of lift of the head like yours.

JEAN Some do and some don't. Some of us walk with turned-out feet—like ducks.

DON Do you?

JEAN (*She walks with turned-out feet to the bench*) Yes.

DON Anyway—

JEAN One day a friend of mine called to say she was coming down here, and suddenly it all seemed kind of trivial. I began to ask myself whether dancing was anything but a narcissistic indulgence.

DON We've all got our egos. Don't you think I get a bang when I hear someone admire a building I designed?

JEAN It's not the same. You created something outside of yourself. You're not a body on display on a stage.

DON My buildings aren't just steel and concrete. They're my mind on display. Art is art, and if it's good, not only is it not narcissistic, it's a boon to the public.

JEAN Maybe I didn't think I was a boon. Anyway, my conscience bothered me enough to—

DON I'm not questioning your conscience. But why, deep down, did you feel so impelled to come? Because your friend did? Because it was the "in" thing to do?

JEAN You're not questioning my conscience. Only my sincerity.

DON No—well, perhaps. Because I'm trying to understand.

JEAN Why did *you* come here tonight?

DON Because I was ashamed not to, I suppose.

JEAN   Which is probably what motivated me. (*She gets up and takes a few steps*) When I was a kid we had a Negro maid. On Saturdays her daughter, who was my age, used to come to spend the day. She always wore hand-me-downs of mine. One Saturday she didn't show. She had pneumonia and she died. I went to the funeral, and though Mother didn't want me to, I had to look in the casket. And of course she was laid out in one of my old party dresses. I can't tell you what that did to me.

DON   I can imagine.

JEAN   It had a lot to do with my coming. And don't think I was so anxious. I felt I should. But I was afraid and unsure and completely miserable. Because if you feel deeply and do nothing, you're really turning your back on what you feel, denying part of your humanity. Am I making sense?

DON   Yes.

JEAN   The funny thing is, I'm teaching a *dance* class! Lou asked me to. And it's become terribly important. I'm still afraid, but I feel much better. If they'd stop killing people, I might even get to like the place.

DON   I'm certainly not apologizing for it.

JEAN   I'm curious. Why, after living in New Haven, did you decide to come back?

DON   For my parents' funeral. And there was the beautiful old house with all the remembered things. Which I didn't have the heart to sell. And it was home. So I stayed. Even though I was pretty lonely as a kid. Used to make up tall stories to amuse myself. But people were considerate, and it seemed like such a friendly place. Very peaceful and quiet. And when Frank offered to take me into the firm— (*There is the sound of a brick shattering a pane of glass*) Duck! On the floor!

(*He sprawls flat, pulling* JEAN *down with him*)

VOICE   The lights! Put out the lights!
(*The stage goes dark except for the moonlight coming in through the shattered window. Another rock crashes in. A swivel spotlight from a car outside shoots in and circles around. It is angled toward the ceiling. We hear yelling and laughter from outside, and then the sound of an auto horn. The spotlight keeps swiveling in crazy arcs*)

VOICES (*Offstage*)   Come on out, you nigger bastards . . . Whyn't you come out and show your baboon faces . . . Hey, you nigger-lovers, what you doin', gettin' you some poontang? . . .
(*Shouts of obscene laughter. Then the sound of a gunshot and sudden silence*)

VOICE   That's what you nigger bastards are gonna get if you march down to the Square tomorrow! We're warning you, now!
(*Laughter is heard again, along with the honk of a horn and a car gunning off*)

JEAN (*Still on the floor*)   You were talking about the peace and quiet.

DON   So I was.
(*He chuckles; she joins him. It grows into laughter tinged with hysteria as the insistent horn of the returning car draws close and another rock crashes*)

25

through the window. The sound of rebel yells rise, then fade as the stage dims into darkness. We hear piano-playing. Lights come up in COFO Center on a group of three Negro teen-age girls in shorts and blouses, their feet bare. JEAN *faces them. They are doing arm swings)*

JEAN Swing, swing and turn around. *One*—two—three; *one*—two—three . . . all right. *(They stop)* Now, remember the improvisation we did yesterday? The earth, the sky, and people all around. Where you made up your movement to the words? *(They nod)* All right. Let's start it the same way, then vary it. I'll throw in a new word now and then, and you do whatever it suggests to you. For instance, the earth, the sky, and *flowers* all around. Clear?

LAURIE Oh, I like that. I can smell 'em.

MAE Or pick 'em.

ANDREA Or scatter 'em. *(Strikes a pose)* Like Queen of the May.

JEAN Right. But first we do it straight. Four counts each for earth, sky, and people all around. *(Piano starts playing)* All right. Heels together, head down, arms come together in circle, fingers touching. *Now* head lifts to sky, arms up in circle overhead. *And* right arm out to side, bend right and left, arm and head. Now, sharper, faster, follow piano . . . Fine. Now anyway you want. The earth, the sky, and people all around. *(Each finds a different movement)* Now. The earth, the sky, and cool winds all around. *(Varied responses)* Now, the earth, the sky, and *sheriffs* all around. *(*ANDREA *moves with dignified disdain,* MAE *backs away,* LAURIE *runs)* All right. The earth, the sky, and *friends* all around. (*Contrasting response in the girls' movement*) Now, the earth, the sky, and *darkness* all around. (*Appropriate reaction in movement*) And. The earth, the sky, and *freedom* all around.

> (*Lovely open movement.* DON, *who has walked into periphery of lighted area and has been watching, is now noticed by* JEAN)

JEAN   Oh, it's you. Hello.

DON   I dropped by to see Lloyd or Lou.

JEAN   They drove to a meeting at state headquarters. But I expect them any minute. Should be back now, actually.

DON   Do you mind if I wait? I don't want to interrupt or be in the way.

JEAN   As a matter of fact, we're about ready to break. Let's just end up with a couple of leaps. First, on the diagonal from the right, and then back from the left. (*The girls go off.* JEAN *picks up a tambourine, pulls out a stool, stands on it, and holds the tambourine high and out*) Ready? Andrea, you start. (ANDREA *runs into lighted area and leaps as she approaches* JEAN, *her hand hitting the tambourine*) Laurie. (*Same procedure*) Mae. (*The same procedure again. Then all three girls repeat the action from the other direction*) Very good. You can go change now.

> (*They exit*)

DON   That looked like fun.

JEAN   It is. They love improvising. There are three others in the class, but they were arrested in yesterday's demonstration.

DON   This thing's getting to be ridiculous. Frank and I talked to some of the businessmen today.

JEAN   And?

DON   They get pale when you mention boycott.

JEAN   Pale enough to talk to the Mayor?

DON   Sam Bassett of the five-and-dime and Leroy Shattuck of the lumber mill are seeing him tonight.

JEAN   Good!

DON   I thought Lloyd and Lou would be pleased.

JEAN   They'll be delighted. I only wish they'd come. (*She glances anxiously at her watch*)

DON   What time were they supposed to be back?

JEAN   Four.

DON   (*Looking at his watch*)   And it's now four-fifty-three.

JEAN   If they don't show by five, I'm supposed to start calling to check.

DON   They were probably held up in traffic.

JEAN   I hope, but I'm worried.

DON   Forget it.

JEAN   I would—except that Betty's with them and she's very strict about time. They all are on the road. Too many things have happened.

(The three girls, who have changed from their shorts, return. They walk through the lighted area)

GIRLS 'Bye, Miss Portugal.

JEAN 'Bye, now. Same time tomorrow.

GIRLS We'll be there.
(They exit. The sounds of the door shutting and their shoes on the stairs are heard)

JEAN I hate to make that call.

DON There's still five minutes.

JEAN I'm glad you're here. If anything's wrong—

DON Don't jump to conclusions. They'll show.

JEAN *(Looking up)* What's that?

DON What? *(We hear hurried footsteps racing down the stairs. DON goes to the door and can be heard opening it)* Whoever it was is gone . . . Oh, he left something.
(He comes back with a folded piece of paper and hands it to JEAN)

JEAN *(Glancing at it)* Valentine. Isn't that charming?
(She hands the note to DON, who reads it)

DON I've seen some pretty obscene things, but that's about the crudest.

JEAN Don't you appreciate the art work?

DON I've seen better on toilet walls.
(He starts to tear it up)

JEAN   Don't tear it. I'm collecting them. Nice memento of a trip to the gallant South. We get a dozen a day. Part of the harassing technique. (*The phone rings;* JEAN *runs to pick it up. It is on a desk, on the fringe of the lighted area*) I hope that's Betty . . . Hello.
(*A loud, almost understandable male voice is heard.* JEAN *listens a moment, then hands the phone to* DON, *whose lips tighten into a grim line at what he hears*)

DON   Listen, you . . . Never mind who I am—sure I sound like a Southerner, because I am one. But I'm ashamed to own up to it when I hear a nasty-minded creep like you—you bastard, don't you call her that!

JEAN   Don't. Don't engage.
(*She takes the phone from him and returns it to the cradle*)

DON   Has this happened before?

JEAN   All the time. Sometimes at two in the morning.

DON   When I think of what I said last night . . . Will you forgive me?

JEAN   For what?

DON   Questioning your motives.

JEAN   Forgiven. It's five. (*Draws in her breath, picks up the phone and dials*) Hello, Roger? This is Jean Portugal in Leucadia. I'm worried. Lou, Betty, and Lloyd were supposed to be back at four. They did leave, didn't they? One. That should have given them ample time. Who? I wish you would. And let me know as soon as you can . . . Thanks, Roger. (*She hangs up*) Damn! Where are they?

DON   Look, all sorts of things might have happened. The car might have conked out. They may be stuck on a roadside waiting for a tow truck.

JEAN   God help them if they are. Because if some Redeemer spots them—(*The phone rings. She snatches it up*) Hello . . . Hello . . . Who is it? Hello! Don't you hear me? (*A click is heard as the silent caller hangs up*) That's another one of their cute little tricks. They call and don't say a word. Just breathe. You can hear them breathe. And then they hang up. And it's maddening! Just maddening!

DON   Take it easy, Jean.
      (*He puts his hand on hers*)

JEAN   If something's happened to them—

DON   Wait till you hear from Roger.
      (*The phone again*)

JEAN   If that's another of those—

DON   Let me take it. (*He picks it up*) Hello. No, it's—
      (JEAN *shakes her head, puts her hand over his mouth, takes the phone*)

JEAN   Hello, Roger. Oh, it's *you*, Betty! I never was so happy to hear anyone's voice in my life. Are you all right? Oh, no! I knew it; I just knew it! I can imagine. But you definitely shook 'em? You're sure. Where are you? No, don't tell me. All right, you work it out and I won't expect to hear from you. No, I won't worry . . . Look, there's no need to be concerned. I'm not alone. So don't even think about it. Give Lloyd and Lou my love. 'Bye. (*She*

turns to DON) They're safe! They're safe! They're safe!
(*She throws her arms around him. He holds her to
him*)

DON   See, you worried for nothing.

JEAN (*Breaking from embrace*)   They were followed, Don.
Someone took a shot. The bullet grazed Lou's head.

DON   The Redeemers. The Supreme Order of White Redeemers . . .

JEAN   I'm scared, Don. I'm so glad you're here. I said that,
didn't I? (*She clings to him a moment, then straightens
up*) All right. Enough of that. I feel better now.

DON   You feel wonderful.
(*She looks at him. Their eyes meet and hold. After a
moment, so do their lips*)

JEAN (*As they come out of their embrace*)   How'd we get
into this?

DON   Does it matter?

JEAN   I suppose not. (*Again they are drawn into a kiss—
long and importunate. The phone's ringing parts them*)
Oh, my God, I forgot all about Roger. (*She picks up the
phone*) Hello. Roger, it's all right! Betty just called. They
did have some trouble. The important thing is that no one
was hurt. I don't know where, and they're not budging for
a while. No, I'm fine . . . Don't worry about me . . .
Right. 'Bye. (*She hangs up*) They're all concerned about
me. Want me to sleep somewhere else tonight.

DON   You can stay at my place.

JEAN   No, someone'd find out and there'd be talk. Not the kind that'd do anyone any good—you or COFO. I'll call Reverend Nichols and ask if I can stay with them. (*She dials and waits*) Funny. Someone should be home.

DON   You can try again later. In the meanwhile, why don't I run out and get something to eat?
　　　(*He starts offstage*)

JEAN   There's no need. There's plenty of food.

DON (*Turning*)   Look, to use one of your favorite expressions, I'm here. Why don't I stay?

JEAN   For the night?

DON   For the night. I'm not going to leave you here alone, that's a cinch.

JEAN   I wouldn't stay alone. The Reverend should be home soon.

DON   It isn't so safe at the Reverend's. They bombed his house once. They might again.

JEAN   They might.

DON   Then why take the chance? (*JEAN looks at him, obviously in conflict*) You're hesitating.

JEAN   Yes. I am.

DON   Why? Are you afraid of me?

JEAN   Not in the sense that you suggest.

DON   Then what's bothering you?

JEAN   Maybe it's that I'm afraid *for* you. For both of us. I have an awful feeling that if we keep seeing each other and get emotionally involved—

DON   I think I already am.

JEAN   I don't want anything to happen to you because of me.

DON   I'm of age. I know what I'm doing.

JEAN   You wouldn't have come here this afternoon if you did.

DON   No one saw me come in.

JEAN   You don't *know* that.

DON   There wasn't a soul on the street.

JEAN   There are buildings, with windows!

DON   Look, I'm not going to let the Redeemers decide whom I can see, or what I can or cannot do.

JEAN   They do, though!

DON   You could come down from New York, but you don't want me to cross the street.

JEAN   It's easier for us, yes. Oh, some of us may get hurt, but after a few weeks or months we leave and are the better for it. But you live here. And when you cross the street—or line—I've seen what they can do. Why'd you have to come, Don!

DON Do you want me to go? Do you want me to leave you here alone? (*She is silent. They stand facing each other*) You don't. And I wouldn't.
(*Another pause. The phone rings.* JEAN, *startled, wheels to pick it up*)

JEAN Hello.
(*She stiffens as the stream of obscenities and threats crackle out of the receiver.* DON *walks over, takes the phone out of her hand. The abuse continues, loud and rasping. A look of rage comes over* DON's *face. He slams the phone back into the cradle*)

DON Those sons a'bitches! Those dirty sons a'bitches!
(JEAN *suddenly breaks into sobs. Solicitously* DON *takes her into his arms to comfort her. The lights dim into darkness. The courthouse clock is striking eight. Lights come up on another area.* DON, *in trousers but stripped to the waist, sits on a chair, putting on his shoes. After a moment* JEAN *enters, dressed in a robe, stretching her arms*)

DON Good morning.
(*He catches hold of her hand as she comes up to him*)

JEAN (*Bending down to kiss him*) Mmm—I haven't slept so soundly in weeks.

DON What you need is me around.

JEAN Apparently . . . I can't decide whether your eyes are brown or hazel.

35

DON   Momentous question.

JEAN   I'm funny that way. Always want to know the color of a man's eyes.

DON   What do you do, keep a journal?

JEAN   Journal?

DON   Of the color of men's eyes.

JEAN   Of course. All I go for, anyway.

DON   Have you gone for many?

JEAN   Why? Are you jealous?

DON   Of every one of them.

JEAN   Everyone comes down to one. His eyes were blue.

DON   I'm properly edified. I don't think I like men with blue eyes.

JEAN   Yours are hazel, I've decided. And they have gold flecks.

DON   Be sure and note that in the journal.

JEAN   Oh, he *is* jealous. (*She rumples his hair*) Silly . . . Blue Eyes turned out to be a stinker, so you have nothing to be jealous about.
      (*She turns. He pulls her to him, holds her a moment, kisses her, then breaks away*)

DON   I've got to get going.

JEAN   What time is it?

DON   Eight-five.

JEAN   Why'd you let me sleep so long?

DON   Because I thought you could use the rest. Besides, you looked too beautiful to wake.

JEAN   I *do* need you around.
(*The pell-mell rush of feet on the stairs is heard.* JEAN *and* DON *turn at the sound. The sounds of a key turning in the lock, then the door being slammed shut follow*)

LOU (*From offstage*)   Jean?

DON   I'm getting out of here.
(*He exits into other room*)

BETTY (*Coming into view*)   Jean?

JEAN   Betty! You're back!
(LOU *and* LLOYD *appear. All are breathless*)

LOU   And damn lucky to get here.

JEAN   Were you followed again?

LOU   In every county.

LLOYD   They must have had it on the Redeemer shortwave.

LOU   The bastards tried to crowd us off the road.

LLOYD   What do you mean, *tried?* Did!

BETTY   If Lloyd hadn't been at the wheel, we'd never have made it.

LLOYD   It's a good thing I did a soup-up job on that motor or we sure wouldn't have.

LOU   They rammed into us at one point. How you pulled out of that one, I'll never know.

LLOYD   Luck.
(They turn at the sound of feet on the stairs. We hear the door open. DEPUTY SHERIFF CLYDE ALLEN *enters with* STEVE CALLOWAY *and* ROY BREWSTER, *young toughs of about twenty-five)*

ROY BREWSTER   That's him. That nigger sittin' there as cool as you please.

DEPUTY SHERIFF ALLEN   On your feet, boy.
(Slowly, his anger obvious, LLOYD *rises)*

STEVE   Yeah, that's them, all right. The nigger was drivin'. Little Blondie was sittin' right next to him, probably rubbin' him up. Had the coon so excited, he sure in hell didn't know where he was.

LOU   I don't think that kind of talk is necessary.

STEVE   And he's the nigger-lovin' Jewboy who was sittin' on the other side of her.

DEPUTY SHERIFF ALLEN   *(Pointing to* LOU *and* LLOYD*)* You and you. I'm takin' you in.
*(*BETTY *goes immediately to* LOU*)*

LOU   For what?

DEPUTY SHERIFF ALLEN   For speeding. Reckless driving. Going through stop signs.

LLOYD   Since I was doing all the driving—

DEPUTY SHERIFF ALLEN   You say somethin', boy?
      (*He steps in toward* LLOYD)

LLOYD   I was saying—

DEPUTY SHERIFF ALLEN   When you're called on to open your mouth, boy, you can speak. Otherwise all I want from you is silence. (*He flicks at a button on* LLOYD'*s shirt, then turns back to* LOU) Now, Jewboy, you asked me what for I was takin' you in and I started to give you the answers when this nigger interrupted. I could give you a dozen reasons but I'll confine myself to one, a very serious offense—and that's hit-and-run drivin'.

LOU   Who hit whom, Sheriff?

DEPUTY SHERIFF ALLEN   A white '60 Impala registered in the name of Lou Marcus of Detroit—that's your name, ain't it, Jewboy?—sideswiped and smashed the left door and fenders of a blue '64 Plymouth Fury, property of Mr. Roy Brewster here.

LOU   The truth of the matter, Sheriff, is the other way around.

ROY BREWSTER   The hell it is! This nigger deliberately ploughed into my car and stepped on the gas and took off.

LLOYD   Now what would I want to do that for?

ROY BREWSTER   Because this Jewboy commie's got you niggers so hopped-up crazy . . .

39

STEVE   This nigger's so hopped-up crazy 'cause Blondie here was rubbin' him up.

LOU   You repeat that once more and so help me—

STEVE   Threats! You heard the Jewboy threaten me, Sheriff.

DEPUTY SHERIFF ALLEN   We had enough trouble outa you two. Now I'm gonna put you away on this hit-and-run charge.

BETTY   I was in that car, Sheriff, and—

ROY   And you're goin' to tell the Sheriff I was crazy enough to smash my brand-new Plymouth Fury into *your* heap, is that it?

BETTY   That's precisely what I'm telling him, yes.

DEPUTY SHERIFF ALLEN   Young lady, I was goin' to do you the courtesy of not includin' you in this arrest. But if you want to come along and—

LLOYD   If you're making an arrest, I was the driver. I don't see why anyone else is involved.

DEPUTY SHERIFF ALLEN   Snap the cuffs on him, Roy.
        (ROY BREWSTER *and* STEVE *grab hold of* LLOYD. BREWSTER *handcuffs him. The* SHERIFF *snaps handcuff on* LOU)

BETTY   Please, Sheriff. He's hurt. Someone took a shot at him.

DEPUTY SHERIFF ALLEN   All right, let's get goin'!
        (*He gives* LOU *a shove.* ROY *pushes* LLOYD. *They*

start out. As soon as they are gone, BETTY *picks up the phone and dials.* DON, *who is now fully dressed, enters from the other room. He makes his way toward the exit)*

JEAN   You'd better wait a moment.

DON   I think I'd better follow. I want to make sure it's the jail they're taking them to.

JEAN   Be careful, Don. Don't let them see you coming out of here.

BETTY   *(Into the phone)* Mr. Lawton, please. Hello, Shirley? This is Betty. Is Jeff still in? Please . . . Hello, Jeff. I'm afraid we need your help again. Deputy Sheriff Clyde Allen just arrested Lou and Lloyd Lewis—on a completely false charge of hit-and-run driving . . . Would you? Please. I'd appreciate it.
   (Lights dim. They then come up on the CHORUS OF COMMENTATORS, *who stand facing the audience in the same tight formation as taken at the beginning of the play)*

FIRST MAN   At eight-forty, Jeff Lawton of Boston, June graduate of Harvard Law and volunteer counsel for CORE, arrived at the county jail.

SECOND MAN   His clients had already been booked, mugged, fingerprinted, and confined.

THIRD MAN   Release on bail was requested.

FIRST MAN   And denied.

FIRST WOMAN   At eight-fifty, the Redeemer shortwave began crackling.

SECOND MAN   Attention! The Jewboy and nigger have been apprehended and taken into custody by Deputy Sheriff Clyde W. Allen.

SECOND WOMAN   At nine-thirteen, Dorrance R. Medford, Grand Wizard of the Supreme Order of Redeemers, dropped by for a visit.

THIRD WOMAN   Other visitors came by.

FIRST MAN   A gallon jug of free-flowing applejack was uncorked.

THIRD MAN   The atmosphere became convivial.

SECOND MAN   Euphoric.

FIRST WOMAN   Sheriff Plunkett circulated around, bent down, squatted on his haunches . . .

SECOND WOMAN   Holding whispered consultations.

THIRD WOMAN   With the men sitting around and telling jokes . . .

FIRST MAN   Color and off-color.

FIRST WOMAN   At five P.M. the men dispersed.

SECOND WOMAN   Going to cars and pickup trucks.

THIRD WOMAN   Silent.

SECOND WOMAN   Preoccupied.

FIRST MAN   At five-one, Deputy Sheriff Clyde W. Allen picked up the phone, said—

SECOND MAN   Get me Mr. Jeff Lawton at the Crescent Motel.

FIRST MAN   Then—

SECOND MAN   Lawton, if you can scratch up two thousand in bail, it may be that I can arrange to have your clients released.

THIRD MAN   When?

SECOND MAN   Now. As soon as you get over.

FIRST WOMAN   At five-thirteen, Attorney Lawton arrived.

SECOND WOMAN   At five-fifteen, the prisoners were released into his custody.

THIRD WOMAN   They walked out into the deserted Square.

FIRST WOMAN   Questioning whether to walk to the Center . . .

SECOND WOMAN   Or drive in Jeff Lawton's car.

THIRD WOMAN   At five-twenty, they got into the car.

FIRST MAN   At five-twenty-six, past the juncture of Columbus and High, a section occupied by warehouses—

SECOND MAN   A moving van jutted out into the street.

FIRST WOMAN   A truck backed out from the driveway of the warehouse opposite.

SECOND WOMAN   Lawton turned the wheel to squeeze through.

THIRD WOMAN   The truck accelerated.

FIRST MAN   Lawton braked, reversed . . .

SECOND MAN   And had to brake again—

THIRD MAN   To avoid collision with a truck which had just turned in from High Street.

FIRST MAN   Cars were parked where none had stood before.

SECOND MAN   One moved forward and pulled up alongside.

FIRST WOMAN   The door swung open.

SECOND WOMAN   A man jumped out, gun in hand.

THIRD WOMAN   He yanked open the door.

FIRST MAN   "Move over," he said.

SECOND WOMAN   Simultaneously, the other door was opened—

THIRD WOMAN   By a man, also armed, who leaped out from the car in back.

FIRST MAN   Cars and trucks which had left the Square at five—

SECOND MAN   Turned in from High . . .

SECOND WOMAN   Quickly . . .

FIRST WOMAN   Efficiently—

THIRD WOMAN   To jam the street—

FIRST WOMAN   And hide from view—

SECOND WOMAN   The transfer of Lou Marcus . . .

THIRD WOMAN   Lloyd Lewis . . .

FIRST WOMAN   And Jeff Lawton—

FIRST MAN   To other cars.

SECOND WOMAN   At five-forty-two, the obstructing truck moved back into the driveway.

FIRST WOMAN   The cars started.

SECOND MAN   The jam broke.

THIRD MAN   The street returned to its normal order.

FIRST MAN   And no one who should not have known knew—

SECOND MAN   That all was not as it should have been.

THIRD MAN   Except for one, Don Tindall.

FIRST WOMAN   Who hadn't actually seen what happened, but . . .

(*A small spot pinpoints* DON, *who stands apart from the* CHORUS)

DON (*To audience*)   I had a fair notion. My office window looks out on the Square facing the courthouse and jail. I was waiting for something to happen and when I saw Jeff Lawton emerge with Lou and Lloyd, I followed. I was stopped by a red light when they crossed High Street. But after the jam broke, I trailed along, far enough behind but keeping the procession in view. On the outskirts of town I saw them turn into Cotillion Road, pass Beauregard Woods, and head up Mount Lamentation. I went as far as I dared, hid my car behind a clump of pines, and continued on foot. I heard their voices, then saw them robed and hooded in the clearing, and saw Lloyd, Lou, and Jeff under heavy guard.
(*Spotlight dims on* DON)

FIRST MAN   There was a ritual that evening.

SECOND MAN   Secret rites for two new Redeemers initiated into the Order.

THIRD MAN   And Supreme Wizard Dorrance R. Medford expatiated on one of his favorite themes.
(MEDFORD, *in white hood and robe, is spotted on a platform.* CHORUS *moves in to face him. They stand in silhouette*)

MEDFORD   God Almighty—

FIRST MAN   He declared.

MEDFORD   Created the universe, created stars and galaxies, moon and earth. He created the wonders of the world and the beauties of Nature. But not in all Nature's diadem

46

will you find a stone so radiant and pure, or in any sunrise or sunset a beauty so sublime, as that of the Southern lady. It is our glory and treasure, and we shall guard it. Guard it from any and all who seek to sully its purity.

CHORUS Amen!

MEDFORD Look at 'em—

SECOND MAN He continued, pointing at the Negro who had been tied to a tree.

MEDFORD Look at that black nigger with his eyes poppin' and dilatin'! Are you scared, boy? Look at those two white niggers—

FIRST MAN He said.

MEDFORD Look at 'em shakin' and quakin' in their pants. Why if we allowed 'em to have their way, you know what we'd be doin'? We'd be openin' the doors of all the cages in all the zoos, we'd be invitin' the beasts from all the jungles, the black apes and gorillas and orang-utans, into the bedrooms and beds of our wives and sisters and daughters. We'd be sayin': Go ahead, you kinky-haired coons, go ahead, you musty-smellin' baboons, throw yourselves on their soft, white bodies, take them in lewd fornication, fill 'em with the dirty seed of your lechery and lasciviousness and lust so they can bring forth a race of mongrelized black bastards!

CHORUS No!

MEDFORD Well, before we let 'em stir up all the black-gummed savages to do their will on us, maybe we'll do our will on them! (CHORUS *shouts its approval with a rebel yell*) What do you say, my fellow Redeemers?

FIRST MAN   His fellow Redeemers had much to say.

SECOND MAN   They said it with swinging clubs.

THIRD MAN   And chains.

FIRST MAN   And bullwhips.

SECOND MAN   They said it with wobbling streams of yellow urine.

THIRD MAN   And with a stainless steel surgical precision razor blade.

FIRST MAN   Which hacked into and removed the black genitalia.

SECOND MAN   One of the three, hearing the black man's screams . . .

THIRD MAN   Broke loose and ran to his aid.
(LOU *tries to help, but is shot. He falls to the ground. There is a moment of silence, after which* JEFF *tries to break away. Another shot blasts out, and* JEFF *falls to the ground*)

DON   I watched, and I too felt a wild impulse to run out and join them. But I didn't. I sat safe in my hiding place and watched them finish the job. One of them, as if to prove his manhood, pumped five shots from a Colt automatic into Lloyd's mangled body, and a couple more ran up to empty their guns. Then all was quiet. A moment ago they were gods, exalting in the power of life and death. Now they were mortals, uneasy. Whatever their thoughts, I had seen their acts. And as they turned to their cars, removing robes and hoods, I could see who they were. And I didn't want to see, didn't want to know! Still, when they loaded the bodies in a truck and started down the hill, I got into my car and followed. I had to.

(*Lights dim out on* DON)

FIRST MAN   It was seven-five when the procession reached the foot of Mount Lamentation.

SECOND MAN   To the right, on the soft shoulder, stood a city sewage bulldozer.

THIRD MAN   All week it had dug into the earth, fashioning a channel for a culvert.

FIRST MAN   Al Burroughs, a Redeemer, ran it.

SECOND MAN   And he mounted the platform to run it now.

THIRD MAN   The area was deserted.

FIRST MAN   And, to make sure it remained so . . .

SECOND MAN   Sheriff Plunkett—

THIRD MAN   And Deputy Sheriff Allen . . .

FIRST MAN   Stationed themselves at intersections a mile apart—

SECOND MAN   To turn away any traffic that might chance that way.

FIRST MAN   By seven-twelve, Al Burroughs had deepened the channel by four feet.

THIRD MAN The bodies were tossed in.

FIRST MAN Unsegregated.

SECOND MAN (*After a pause*) Returning that evening . . .

FIRST MAN Fortified with more applejack . . .

THIRD MAN The Redeemers decided to round off the evening by stopping in at the Redhead's.
(*A barrelhouse piano is heard*)

SECOND MAN They filed into the whorehouse.

THIRD MAN Making for the brown-skin girls.
(WOMEN *in the* CHORUS *run offstage with mock screams*)

FIRST MAN Shouting, "Poontang!"

SECOND AND THIRD MEN "We want poontang!"
(*Men run offstage after the women. Lights dim. The sound of the piano swells, then recedes. Lights come up on* COFO *Center.* BETTY *sits at the desk with a pad and pencil.* SARAH COLLINS, *a Negro girl, is typing.* JEAN *is working on the mimeograph.* ROGER COLLINS, *a Negro of about thirty, is stacking the mimeographed sheets.* SARAH *stops typing at the sound of a knock on the door. All watch as* ROGER *goes to answer it*)

ROGER Who is it?

DON (*Offstage*) Don Tindall.

JEAN It's all right. He's a friend. (*We hear a key turn in the lock and a door opening.* DON *enters lighted area with*

ROGER) Hi. This is Roger and Sarah Collins . . . Don Tindall. Roger's state head of COFO.

DON (*Nods, shakes hands with* ROGER) Glad to know you. I'm pleased to see the girls aren't alone.

ROGER That was our general idea in coming down here.

BETTY And we didn't discourage it . . . You know that they refused to release Lou and Lloyd on bail.

DON (*Uneasily*) No, I didn't . . .

BETTY I only hope they didn't put Lou in a cell with a bunch of rednecks. Because if they gang up on you—

ROGER Lou can take care of himself.

JEAN And it isn't as if it's the first time he's been in jail.

SARAH If I know Lou, he's got 'em telling him their life stories.

BETTY (*Sighing*) Well, there's no sense thinking about it . . . Jean, why don't you ask Don if he'd like a piece of that chocolate cake?

JEAN And there's coffee.

DON I'd like the coffee.
(JEAN *takes* DON's *hand and leads him stage left. Lights dim on* BETTY, *and come up on a table and chairs. As they come into lighted area,* JEAN *turns to him and they kiss*)

JEAN You really shouldn't have come.

DON I had to make sure that the two of you weren't on your own. Jean—

JEAN What? (*He shakes his head*) What's wrong, Don?

DON Nothing . . .

JEAN You look as though there is. Your face was white when you came in.

DON I'm all right.

JEAN You'd better sit down. (*He does so*) I'll heat up the coffee.
(*The lights come up on* BETTY. *The phone on the desk rings, and she picks it up*)

BETTY Hello. Yes, Shirley. No, he isn't here. Was he supposed to be? When was this? At five! Good God, it's after seven. Lou would surely have come right back. Or called. I don't have the faintest idea where. If Jeff had the car, they might have dropped Lloyd at his place. I'll call and see. Though I'm not going to tell Anne. Why scare her?— Right.
(*She hangs up, her hand still on the receiver.* JEAN *and* DON, *during the phone conversation, have returned*)

JEAN What happened?

BETTY The Sheriff phoned Jeff to show with bail. At five.

ROGER The question is—are they out or are they still there?

BETTY I can call the Sheriff.

ROGER Call Anne first.

BETTY (*Dials*) Hello, Anne. Betty. As one jail widow to another, I wanted to know how things were going. Did you get hold of Lloyd's sister? I'm glad she's with you. Yes, Jean's here and Roger drove down with Sarah . . . Nothing new. You'll know when there is . . . 'Bye.
(*She hangs up, shaking her head*)

ROGER Well, I guess you'd better call the Sheriff.
(BETTY *picks up the phone and dials*)

BETTY May I speak to the Sheriff, please. Sheriff, this is Betty Marcus at COFO. I've been told my husband and Mr. Lewis were supposed to be released. They were? When? . . . But it's almost three hours since and there's been no sign or word. And that includes Mr. Lawton and Mr. Lewis, whose wives I've talked to . . . No, Sheriff, my husband knew I was worried. He wouldn't have gone anywhere without calling . . . I doubt that.

ROGER (*Taking the phone*) This is Roger Collins, Sheriff. And this call is intended to notify you that we consider Lou Marcus, Lloyd Lewis, and Jeff Lawton to be missing, and we expect you to take action on it. I have witnesses here who are noting the time of this call, and I hold you responsible if anything does happen. Don't put me off, Sheriff, because we're calling the FBI, the Justice Department, and the press. No, I'm not looking for trouble. I don't have to . . . Thanks.
(*He hangs up*)

JEAN Is he going to do anything?

ROGER He says he'll send out a missing call. Who does he think he's kidding. If anything did happen, you can be sure he was in on it.

53

BETTY   You think something did, don't you, Roger?

SARAH   How does *he* know? You had to open your fat mouth!

ROGER   I said "if."

SARAH   Why don't you keep your ifs to yourself?

BETTY   We've got to face the possibility, Sarah.

JEAN   We do. But let's not jump to conclusions.

BETTY   What do you think, Don?

DON (*Obviously disturbed*)   I don't know what to think.

BETTY   If that damn Sheriff handed them over to the Redeemers—

JEAN   It's not very likely.

BETTY   Why not? I can't think of anything more likely.

JEAN   Because things're already too hot. Because there's a spotlight on this town. He wouldn't dare.

BETTY   He'd dare. And I think we have to proceed on the assumption that he would.

JEAN   It could be that Lloyd picked up a bottle of corn to celebrate.

SARAH   And they're probably sitting over it right now.

BETTY   Let's not tell each other fairy tales. Roger doesn't think so. And neither does Don, who knows the white mentality of this town. You know the Sheriff, don't you, Don?

DON   Yes, I know him.

BETTY   And? (*The phone rings; she picks it up*) Hello
. . . (*There is a pause, with* BETTY *listening to what the
caller is saying. Suddenly she loses control and starts
shouting into the phone*) Shut up! Shut your dirty, filthy
mouth! You monsters! You murderers! *Will you shut up!!*
(*She slams down the phone. There is a moment of silence
as she pulls herself together*) That was a stupid thing to
do. Why am I wasting my energy on them?
   (ROGER *picks up the phone and starts to dial. The
lights dim quickly, except for a spot which pinpoints
his face. We hear a phone ringing. Another spot
picks up the face of* STANLEY REEVES. *The light
source for all of the callers who follow is a pen flash-
light in each phone, or handheld and pointed up at
their faces*)

REEVES   Hello.

ROGER   Mr. Reeves? This is Roger Collins at the COFO
Center. We need your help. Lou Marcus and Lloyd
Lewis were released into the custody of Jeff Lawton at
five-seventeen. There's been no trace of them since.

REEVES   Did you call the Sheriff?

ROGER   Yes. But he doesn't seem very concerned.

REEVES   I'll talk to him and go on from there.
   (*Blackout. We hear a phone ring. Lights from pen
flashlights come up on the faces of* REEVES *and the*

SHERIFF, *standing at opposite sides of the stage, phones in their hands*)

REEVES Sheriff? Reeves. What's the story on the two COFO boys and their attorney? I'm told they're missing.

SHERIFF They're either piss-eyed drunk or in a cathouse. If they don't get in by morning, I'll consider 'em missing.

REEVES I wouldn't dismiss it that lightly, Sheriff.

SHERIFF Boys'll be boys, Counselor.

REEVES Are you sure someone didn't tip off the Redeemers that you were releasing them? And are you sure the Redeemers didn't pick 'em up?

SHERIFF Look, if you're implying—

REEVES All I'm saying is that if anything happens to those boys, it's going to be damn serious.

SHERIFF What am I supposed to do, search the cathouses?

REEVES You know what you're supposed to do, Sheriff.
(*Blackout. Ringing of another phone. Lights in phones pinpoint the faces of* REEVES *and the* MAYOR)

REEVES Mr. Mayor, I know you're concerned about the image of this city. It's in a bad way now. But if something happens to those boys . . .

MAYOR I'll do my best, Counselor.
(*Blackout. Ringing again. Lights now spot the faces of the* MAYOR *and* SHERIFF)

MAYOR You've caused me enough trouble, Sheriff. Now I want you to get on this and get on it fast.

SHERIFF If you want me to put out a missing call—

MAYOR I want you to get out every law enforcement officer in the county. We've got to find those boys!
(*Blackout. Ringing. Lights spot faces of the* SHERIFF *and* AL BURROUGHS)

SHERIFF Now you listen to me. Every man on that road crew's a Redeemer. And I expect 'em to be out there in half an hour pourin' a nice, thick layer of cement on that culvert.

AL Supposin' somebody comes by.

SHERIFF Ain't nobody comin' because the road's goin' to be blocked off at both ends for repairs. And it's goin' to be blocked off tomorrow. Got it?

AL Got it.
(*Blackout. Ringing again. Lights on* SHERIFF *and a* REPORTER)

REPORTER Frank Aldridge of the *New York Times.* Do you have a statement on the missing boys, Sheriff?

SHERIFF Who says they're missing? Is every man who plays hookey from his wife for four hours missing?

REPORTER That's what the report says.

SHERIFF Well, if they're missing, it's because they planned it. They disappeared to give the impression they been kidnapped and done away with. They came from up North to give this town a black eye, and this is just another way of doin' it.

(Blackout. There are now several phones ringing. Lights from pen flashlights come up on the actors' faces. A murmur becomes audible, through which stray phrases can be heard above the ringing phones)

VOICES I can assure you we're doing everything in our power . . . Every law enforcement agency of this county has been alerted and mobilized . . . It's a hoax, a deliberate conspiracy to defame the good name of this state . . . Have every confidence they will return before morning . . . Attorney General's office calling . . . I take it very seriously, sir. Knowing the working relationship between the Sheriff and the Redeemers, I very much fear . . . Do you have a statement, Governor? . . . Deplore and decry lawlessness, abhor violence . . . Cannot believe that this alleged disappearance is anything but a monstrous fraud . . . A base, communist-inspired deception . . . Got to find those boys! . . . The image of this town . . . Campaign to attract industry . . . Cannot believe . . . Fraud . . . Hoax . . . Fraud!

(The voices and ringing of phones mount to a climax, then come to an abrupt halt. A spotlight picks out DON, *stage front)*

DON I stayed up all night with the others as they waited for some word, some clue. I was tempted to come out with it. But I couldn't tell Betty. I didn't have the heart. Couldn't even tell Jean. Not only out of concern for them. I was concerned about a hundred things. All the repercussions that might follow and which I wasn't prepared to face. The more I thought about it, the more frightening was my realization that I was the only non-Redeemer who knew, the only witness, should it come to that, who could tell.

(*The lights fade*)

Curtain

Act Two

The curtain rises on the CHORUS OF COMMENTATORS *spotlighted in the same tight grouping.*

FIRST WOMAN   A hoax.

SECOND WOMAN   A trick.

FIRST MAN   A conspiracy to sully the fair name of this state . . .

SECOND MAN   The Governor continued to say.

THIRD WOMAN   So, too, did the Mayor—

THIRD MAN   Sheriff—

FIRST WOMAN   Police—

SECOND MAN   And the man on the street.

FIRST MAN   Nonetheless.

FIRST WOMAN   To allay all doubt.

FIRST MAN   Squads of police, sheriffs, possemen and militia . . .

SECOND MAN   Were ordered to maintain diligent search.

63

FIRST WOMAN There were those who said their diligence was confined—

SECOND WOMAN To close observation of the search conducted by—

FIRST MAN The FBI, Justice Department, and units of the U.S. Marines.

FIRST WOMAN Search parties beat the bush, dragged the river, waded, hip-booted, through the swamps.

THIRD MAN And out of the swamps they dredged two black bodies reported missing months before.

SECOND MAN They found, also, an assortment of stray arms and legs.

FIRST WOMAN But no trace of the missing three.

FIRST MAN For all the alien intrusions and momentary alarms.

SECOND MAN The town pursued its customary ways.

SECOND WOMAN Confident that the search would come to a fruitless end.

THIRD MAN As had the demonstrations in Constitution Square.

FIRST MAN For this was Fair time.

THIRD MAN The biggest, brightest, gayest, and most fabulous County Fair of the Southland!

(Calliope music is heard. CHORUS *breaks formation to become spectators at the Fair)*

SECOND MAN   Yessir! Step right up and take a trip in a spaceship! See the moon! Mars! Venus!

FIRST MAN   See it! See it! See it! Marvel the Magician! See him saw a woman, not in two—but in four. Yes, in four, ladies and gentlemen!

THIRD MAN   Hot dogs here! Hot dogs!

SECOND MAN   Tonight! Tonight at eight! The big event! Watch the judges make their final selection for Beauty Queen of the Year! Come one, come all! Witness the crowning of the loveliest of the lovely!

FIRST WOMAN   That day, after Willie Winters had won the pie-eating contest by wolfing down thirty-four blueberry pies . . .

THIRD MAN   And Piggy Adams had been awarded the hog-calling championship . . .
    (Hog calls)

FIRST MAN   Just as Sally Popper, bosom thirty-seven, waist twenty-four, hips thirty-seven, was sashaying across the stage, her clearly defined buttocks swiveling sassily . . .
    (A girl from the CHORUS *illustrates action)*

SECOND MAN   Word came.
    *(CHORUS *falls back into tight formation)*

FIRST WOMAN   That a car.

SECOND WOMAN   With a Massachusetts license.

65

SECOND MAN   Belonging to attorney Jeff Lawton.

THIRD MAN   Had been discovered.

FIRST MAN   Overturned and burned down to the metal.

FIRST WOMAN   On a swamp road in Fern County, thirty miles below Leucadia ...
(*Lights dim on* CHORUS. *To the right a light has come up on* DON, *who stands over a drafting table,* FRANK *beside him*)

DON   And thirty-five miles south of the Beauregard culvert.

FRANK   Funny thing about that car. Everything on it that could possibly take fire, including the tires, burned. But the grass around it didn't.

DON   Maybe it's fireproof.

FRANK   Maybe they're being a little overconfident. Obviously it was transported from somewhere else.

DON   Good deductive reasoning. Doesn't tell you from where though, does it?

FRANK   I think that was the object.

DON   Want me to tell you?

FRANK   I don't see how you could.

DON   What if I were to tell you I know where, how, and by whom it was done?

FRANK   You haven't—and I wouldn't hear you if you did.

DON   Let's suppose for a moment that I did.

FRANK   It's a very dangerous supposition.

DON   Nonetheless, *if* I did—

FRANK   You didn't! You heard nothing and saw nothing and know nothing.

DON   Would that be your attitude?

FRANK   It's mine. And it's yours. It's got to be. Because we live in this town, we grew up here. It's our life, yours and mine. And for all that's bad, there's more that's good.

DON   Did you ever see a Negro get the full treatment? See his genitals chopped off? See three men shot?

FRANK   No. And neither did you. *Neither did you, Don . . .*

DON   Let's say I had a very bad dream.

FRANK   Let's say you did. And let's forget about it, here and now.

DON   It's wrong, Frank.

FRANK   In my book death is always wrong.

DON   I was talking about silence.

FRANK   I could argue that.

DON   So could the Germans.

FRANK   This is the South, U.S.A. Suppose someone *did* know and talked. In this atmosphere, with everyone worked up, would there be an indictment? And if there were, would there be a trial? Would a jury find anyone guilty?

DON   Probably not.

FRANK   So what's been accomplished? Justice—or justification?
    (*He walks offstage*)

DON (*To audience*)   There was a certain validity in Frank's argument. But that didn't relieve me of the responsibility of doing what I knew I should. I worked myself up to the point of going to a phone booth. I dialed Stanley Reeves of the Justice Department. But for all my bravado, I didn't give my name and I told only part of the story— just the location of the bodies. I didn't have to disguise my voice—it had such a tremor in it. The phone was ringing when I got home. It was Gwen. Would I see her? What was the point? I asked. There was something she had to tell me, something I ought to know. She pleaded with me to come over, said I might regret it if I didn't. She sounded wild and desperate, so I finally said I would.
    (*The lights, which have started to dim on* DON, *are now out. The sound of a piano is heard again. Lights come up on* GWEN, *who is playing a Rachmaninoff Prélude. After a moment* DON *walks into the lighted area. He stands listening until she suddenly realizes his presence and breaks off abruptly*)

DON   You always play well when you're upset.

GWEN   I didn't even hear the bell. (*She looks up expectantly*) Aren't you going to kiss me?

68

DON You had something to tell me.

GWEN I do. But that doesn't mean you can't be civil.

DON I don't mean to be uncivil. (*He leans over and kisses her on the cheek*) But I don't want to pretend either.

GWEN I appreciate that. (*Indicating a place on the bench beside her*) Sit down, Don.

DON (*Sitting beside her*) I wrote you what I felt.

GWEN I don't blame you for holding last week against me.

DON It isn't a matter of last week.

GWEN But I was wrong. It wasn't till the disappearance of those boys that I realized how wrong. Now that they've found the car and may find the bodies, I know what bad taste it'd be to have a public wedding. I wish now we'd gone off by ourselves.

DON It's lucky we didn't.

GWEN You were the one who wanted it.

DON Or thought I did. Deep down, although we may not have acknowledged it, I think we both knew it wasn't very real.

GWEN I didn't. I don't think you did. Until you met her.

DON (*Looking up*) What does that mean?

GWEN Simply that. You're not denying that there is a "her"?

DON No. But I wrote that letter *before* I met her.

GWEN Out of anger. Because you felt I was pressing you. And I was. I pressured you right into her arms. Is she pretty?

DON I really don't see any point to this, Gwen. If you have something to tell me—

GWEN Yes, I have. I want to warn you. You're not being very smart. Not in going to that Center. And not in getting involved with that nigger-lovin' dancer from New York.

DON Is that it?

GWEN You're in trouble, Don. I'm not the only one who knows.

DON You're talking about that brother-in-law of yours, I take it?

GWEN No, I had a visit from Mrs. Plunkett. The Sheriff told her. You should've known that every inch of that place'd be bugged.

DON We have an efficient Sheriff.

GWEN Don't be sarcastic. He's being very considerate about it.

DON How? By telling you?

GWEN By not telling anyone else. In spite of everything, he happens to like you. And the Plunketts are very fond of Mama. They're counting on me to bring you back to your senses.

DON   Which means what?

GWEN   That you forget about this past week, forget our silly little quarrel, forget that girl.

DON   And we go right ahead with the wedding, is that it?

GWEN   It doesn't have to be a church wedding. I'll do whatever you want.

DON   The situation's changed, Gwen.

GWEN   You said you loved me. Can you honestly say we weren't happy with each other?

DON   Of course we were—at first.

GWEN   Always. I'd have known if you weren't. Would you have written that letter if we hadn't quarreled?

DON   Probably not.

GWEN   Then why can't we get married? Mama never did do anything about those invitations, so everybody expects us to anyway.

DON   The question isn't what people expect, Gwen.

GWEN   No. But what are we to do? Let everyone come and then announce the groom walked out on me?

DON   All Mama has to do is get on the phone and tell everyone I turned out to be a nigger-lover, and under the circumstances you called it off. You'd come out smelling like a rose.

GWEN This isn't a joke. If you're not going to be sensible, then I can't guarantee the Sheriff won't talk.

DON And I'll get a nice visit from the Redeemers . . .

GWEN If my brother-in-law has anything to say about it, you will.

DON (*Turning*) Is that a threat?

GWEN It's a fact. And the only one who can change it is you. (DON *is silent*) Is the idea so repulsive to you?

DON It wouldn't work, Gwen. It just wouldn't.

GWEN (*Going to him*) You used to think I was attractive. You couldn't keep your hands off me.
(*She steps in close, her body touching his*)

DON I still think you are.

GWEN Then why? All right, you don't want marriage. What's wrong with going on as we were?

DON Nothing, except—

GWEN (*Turning sharply*) Except that you're already getting it from her, so why do you need me? Is she so irresistible? She's probably sleeping with every buck nigger who hangs around that place.

DON Look, Gwen—

GWEN What do you think those Northern bitches come down here for? They're screaming crazy for it!

DON   Cut it, Gwen.

GWEN   You think you'll be any good to her if the Redeemers get you up in the hills? (DON *turns and starts walking away*) What're you going to do? (DON *is silent. She follows him*) Don't be a damn fool, Don!
(*He doesn't respond. She turns and, with a sob, runs offstage.* DON *begins to walk out of scene as lights dim. A spotlight comes up on him as he stops beside an armchair, and a side table on which a phone is situated*)

DON   (*To the audience*) I didn't know what I was going to do. I couldn't get away fast enough. (*He drops into the armchair*) When I got home, I put a record on, poured myself a drink, and tried to think it out. I did a lot of thinking, but couldn't come up with any answers. At least none that would allow me to stay in town, go on with work, and keep my skin intact.
(*He picks up the phone and dials. Ringing is heard. A spotlight picks up* FRANK *as he answers the phone. He is seated in a chair on the other side of the stage*)

FRANK   Hello.

DON   Frank. I've got an announcement to make . . .   I'm leaving the firm.

FRANK   That's quite an announcement.

DON   You'll have my formal resignation tomorrow.

FRANK   I won't accept it.

DON   I think you will.

73

FRANK   There's some reasoning behind this, I take it?

DON   The climate of this town no longer agrees with me.

FRANK   All right now, let's level. You haven't done anything foolish, have you?

DON   Apparently. I fell in love.

FRANK   And I have an invitation to the wedding. What's that got to—

DON   With another girl.

FRANK   That *is* foolish.

DON   Who teaches dancing to Negro children.

FRANK   At the COFO Center. Oh, you idiot! Does Gwen know?

DON   Yes.

FRANK   Who else?

DON   The Sheriff. They're giving me a chance to come to my senses.

FRANK   Then what's the problem?

DON   You know how long that marriage would last? A week. And word'd get around—and it wouldn't do me any good, or the firm. Which is why I'm getting out and you're calling the *Post* to take an ad to announce it.

FRANK   Don't be a horse's ass. If you'd spilled your guts about the three boys, which is what I assumed, that'd be one thing. But this is correctable. Use your head, man.

DON Call the *Post* and place the ad, Frank. (*He hangs up. The lights dim out on* FRANK) For a moment I had the feeling I was making a terrible mistake and I sat debating whether I ought to call Gwen. Then I jumped to the other extreme and began telling myself I really *should* go in and tell everything I knew. I wondered whether that anonymous phone call had meant anything, whether they'd even act on it. I wanted to tell Jean, to talk it out with her. But how could I? What was I going to do, ask her whether I should risk my neck when she was risking hers every day of the week? Oh, you're a brave specimen, Tindall. A bush-league Hamlet pondering yes, no, and maybe; weighing each if, but, and therefore. To act or not to act, that is the question. I asked myself a thousand times and answered: yes, no, maybe . . .

> (*He sighs, and lets his head sink back against the cushioning of the chair. The music continues in background. Voices of the* CHORUS *come out of the darkness. A dim spotlight remains focused on* DON)

FIRST VOICE You sent the five twenties. Why didn't you leave well enough alone, Tindall?

SECOND VOICE Did you have to go and get yourself involved?

THIRD VOICE If you'd used your head, you'd have known the place was bugged.

FIRST VOICE Did you have to spend the night there?

THIRD VOICE Why? Did you think it was more romantic with a dancer?

SECOND VOICE Love? Oh, that makes it even more romantic.

FIRST VOICE Love, love, love. The ruler of the universe is love, love, love.
(*We hear the banging of a gavel*)

SECOND VOICE Oyez! Oyez! Oyez!

THIRD VOICE Do you swear to tell the truth, the whole truth and nothing but the truth, so help you God?

DON (*Who has risen from the armchair*) Yes, no, maybe.

THIRD VOICE Be seated.
(DON *sits*)

FIRST VOICE Did you, on the night of July 16, have carnal knowledge of a Caucasian female in the fifth ballet position?

DON Yes, no, maybe.

FIRST VOICE I see . . . Do you believe in the mongrelization of the white race?

DON Equally with the black.

FIRST VOICE Are you a mongrel?

DON Arf! Arf!

FIRST VOICE Would you like to see your sister marry a—

DON Arf! Arf!

SECOND VOICE I now show you exhibit 393-4096. Do you recognize it?

DON Yes, no, maybe.

SECOND VOICE It is, as you will note, a picture of three bodies, two Caucasian, one African in origin. Can you name them?

DON Homo sapiens, Homo sapiens, and Homo sapiens.

SECOND VOICE And you last saw them?

DON When the moon came over the mountain.

SECOND VOICE What were they doing?

DON Breathing.

SECOND VOICE Were they not in fact beaten, shot, and buried while you remained silent and looked on?
    (*Back lighting silhouettes the figures of* LLOYD, LOU, *and* JEFF. *Their voices have an unearthly sound*)

LLOYD Why did you look on, Don?

LOU Why didn't you do something?

JEFF Why didn't you stop them?

FIRST VOICE Objection! Corpses are not allowed to talk in courtrooms.

JUDGE Objection overruled. Witness will answer the questions.

77

LLOYD   Why didn't you, Don?

DON   I couldn't.

LOU   Why not?

DON   I would have been shot. I wouldn't have been able to testify.

LLOYD   Then why don't you?

LOU   Yes, why don't you, Don?

LLOYD, LOU, and JEFF   *Why don't you testify, Don?*
> (*The light blacks out on* LLOYD, LOU, *and* JEFF. *A shaft of lights cuts across the stage. An organ playing "Here Comes the Bride" is heard.* GWEN *in her wedding gown, holding onto the arm of* STEVE, *who is robed in Redeemer garb, is followed by a procession of robed Redeemers as she walks toward the* JUDGE. *Two robed figures come to* DON *to escort him. A whisper of "sensible, sensible, sensible, sensible" starts and grows as they walk toward the* JUDGE. *The* JUDGE *raises his hand. There is a moment of silence*)

JUDGE   For as much as Don Tindall and Gwen Grayson have consented together in holy wedlock and witnessed the same before God and this company, and whereas and whereof and other facts pertaining thereto, I do, by the authority vested in me, now declare them to be man and wife. You may kiss the bride.
> (*The crowd applauds.* DON *and* GWEN *turn to each other and kiss, then turn full front as if to proceed up the aisle.* GWEN's *face is black. The applause stops dead; the music of a waltz is heard.* JEAN *dances into*

the lighted area. She pauses before DON, *holding out her hands. Together they dance around the stage in the light of a follow spot. To the rear the reflection of red flames is seen. There is a murmur of "Fire! Fire!" which is picked up. The stage is suddenly alive with running figures who flee away from the flames. In the panic the* JUDGE, REDEEMERS *and* GWEN *run offstage.* JEAN *and* DON *continue dancing, oblivious. After a moment, as they near the armchair, they stop and* DON *drops into the chair. The music becomes dissonant and dramatic.* JEAN's *dancing adapts to it. First she moves away from the flames, then toward them. As she nears them,* DON, *who is still seated, suddenly seems to notice them. He tries to warn her, but no sound comes out of his mouth; he tries to get up, but can't. The flames seem to envelop* JEAN's *body as she dances offstage. A cry of "Jean! Jean!" suddenly tears out of* DON's *throat as he obviously comes out of his dream. The music has stopped. He looks around, bewildered. The flames are still evident and now their realistic crackle can be heard, along with the crash of a roof caving in. Sheets of flame accompany these sounds.* DON *gets up, shields his face with his arm, and takes a few steps toward the flames, which come from a wing of the house. He turns back, and rushes to pick up the phone)*

DON Operator! This is an emergency! I want to report a fire on 36 Maple Street.

(Fast dim as DON *runs offstage. A fire alarm and then fire engine sirens are heard. Lights come up on* BETTY, JEAN, SARAH, *and* ROGER *at the Center. They are as absorbed as they were in the last Center scene, with* BETTY *at the desk,* SARAH *typing,* JEAN *turning*

the mimeograph, and ROGER *stacking. A knock on the door is heard. Roger goes to answer it*)

DON'S VOICE (*Offstage*) It's me. Don.
(*We hear the sound of the lock, then of the door opening. A moment later he enters the lighted area. He carries a framed canvas under one arm, a portfolio under the other*)

ROGER You look like you're moving in.

DON I don't have much choice.

JEAN I thought you were going to stay home and get a decent night's sleep.

DON I had a good thirty minutes'. And I guess that was twenty too many. Because the house was half burned down when I woke.

JEAN Oh, Don . . .

DON The Redeemers never did cultivate a taste for good architecture.

ROGER Or people.

DON Any word?
(ROGER *shakes his head*)

BETTY Another contingent of troops was flown in.

DON (*Sighs*) Where'll I park this stuff?

BETTY Right there, for the time being.

DON (*Putting down his things*)   I managed to salvage my drawings. Thought they might fill up the walls. And my Chagall. Isn't that nice?
(*He holds it up*)

JEAN   Lovely.

DON   And a photo album. Look.
(*He riffles through to a page*)

JEAN   It looks like Lloyd.

DON   At the age of six.

ROGER   Bright face.

BETTY   Those beautiful eyes . . .

DON   Is there a way up to the roof? I want to see the last flames. Watch the phoenix rise . . .

BETTY   The stairs go right up.

DON   Anybody want to come along . . . Jean?
(JEAN *turns. Fast dim on the Center. Lights up on rooftop near a cutout of the chimney. A red glow from the fire is reflected on right side of the cyclorama.* JEAN *and* DON, *hand-in-hand, stop beside the chimney and stand looking toward the fire*)

JEAN   Funny how something so ugly can look so beautiful.

DON   It'll look ugly enough in the morning.

JEAN   I heard the sirens, I knew there was a fire, and I didn't make the slightest connection.

DON   Why should you?

JEAN   Because I had a call from a Mrs. Emily Grayson this afternoon.

DON   Mama. I should have anticipated that.

JEAN   She asked if I knew I was breaking up a marriage.

DON   How can you break up a marriage that doesn't exist?

JEAN   She was furious. Asked me to think it over because she was afraid her son-in-law, who's a Redeemer, might find out about it. And apparently he did. I feel awful.

DON   It had nothing to do with you.

JEAN   I tried to call you, but you weren't in the office or at home.

DON   I was at Gwen's. It was what I said to her that brought Steve and the Redeemers into it.

JEAN   What are you going to do, Don?

DON   I don't know, now that the house is gone . . . Tindalls have lived in that house since 1789.

JEAN   That must mean a great deal to you.

DON   It used to. I should get angry at the cretins who did it. But at least it gives me a reason for leaving the town.

JEAN   I think you should leave. I think you should take the first train out.

DON   Would you go with me?

JEAN   I'd like to. But I can't. Not now. I can't walk out on Betty.

DON   But I can? Why doesn't that apply to me?

JEAN   Because I don't want to find out one day that you too are missing, and have to wait like Betty to hear your body's been dredged out of a swamp. That's a horrible thing to say, but it's in my mind. It's what I'm thinking.

DON   It's what they want you to think.

JEAN   It's not just my imagination, Don. They burned your house. There's a six-fifteen train in the morning. I want you to promise me you'll be on it.

DON   I can't walk out on you any more than you can on Betty.

JEAN   It isn't the same. I'm *sending* you. Don't be such a gallant Southern gentleman!

DON   If I were, I'd marry Gwen.

JEAN   Maybe you should.

DON   Do you mind if I don't?

JEAN   No. I'd hate you if you did.
       (*They stand looking at each other a moment, then kiss.* DON *puts his arm around her as they turn to look out at the fire*)

DON   The flames seem to be dying down.

83

JEAN   Do you see the phoenix?

DON   The Redeemers probably clipped its wings.

JEAN   Silly. (*Her head rests against his shoulder. They stand in silence a moment. It is interrupted by an anguished cry. A tight spot hits* BETTY *as the cry wrenches out of her.* JEAN *recognizes the voice*) Betty . . . It's Betty!
      (*They start for the stairway as the scene blacks out. Lights come up in the Center.* BETTY *is weeping, her face in her hands.* SARAH *tries to comfort her.* ROGER *stands at her side. Facing them in profile is* STANLEY REEVES, *a neatly dressed man.* JEAN *and* DON *come onstage*)

JEAN   What is it? What happened?

BETTY   (*Looking up. She tries to keep her voice steady*) This is Mr. Reeves, of the Justice Department. They found them. They found their bodies . . .
      (*Her voice breaks*)

JEAN   No.
      (*She runs to* BETTY, *trying to console her. Her arm goes around her*)

BETTY   I knew. From the moment Shirley called to ask if Jeff was here, I knew. There were only the details to fill in. Now they are. Do you know where the bodies were buried, Jean? Under the new culvert, just before the concrete was poured. Everything perfectly planned, timed, and executed. Damn them! God damn them!
      (*Her voice breaks*)

JEAN   Betty . . . Don't, Betty.

DON (*To* REEVES, *after a pause*)   Do you have any idea who actually . . .

REEVES   We've got a very good idea. There's been a lot of bragging about this glorious deed. Not that anyone's going to talk. Not to the Department, not to the FBI, and least of all, in court.

BETTY   Are you going to *bring* the case to court?

REEVES   That's under the jurisdiction of the state. You know that, Betty.

BETTY   I know that the state's not going to do a thing about it—and so do you!

REEVES   Let's wait and see, Betty.

BETTY   I'm asking *you*, Stanley Reeves, whether the Department of Justice is going to seek justice against the murderers of Lou Marcus, Lloyd Lewis, and Jeff Lawton!

REEVES   The Department and the FBI will co-operate with the state by turning over all information and evidence.

ROGER   Which will be utterly disregarded. Officers of this state are involved, Mr. Reeves. The Sheriff and Deputy Sheriff of the county are involved. Do you expect the murderers to indict, prosecute, and convict themselves?

REEVES   We're a nation of law, Mr. Collins. And we've got to proceed by the law.

ROGER   Is the law so infallible? A President of the United States is assassinated in Texas. He's President of all the states, but the one state has jurisdiction. Does that make sense?

REEVES Not too much, no.

ROGER The Federal Government has the power to send our boys abroad to fight and die. But let three boys be killed in this town and the Federal Government hasn't got a thing to say about it. The Federal Government isn't concerned.

REEVES It's very much concerned.

BETTY But the state has jurisdiction! A state in which no white man who's ever killed a Negro or civil rights worker has ever been convicted! Oh, we're a nation of law, all right! But what kind of law is it? (*A sob breaks in her throat*) I don't know why I'm beating up on you. It's not your fault, and I know where your heart is. I'm sorry.

REEVES (*After a pause*) Do you think you'll be up to driving over to identify Lou's body?

JEAN Does she have to? I can go. Any one of us can.

BETTY I'll go. I want to see him no matter what he looks like. But before I do I've got something to take care of that may be just as rough. (*She picks up phone and dials for the operator*) Operator. I want to make a person-to-person call to Detroit, Michigan. The name of the party is Marcus. (*Her voice breaks*) Mr. David Marcus.
(*Lights dim out. Lights come up on the* CHORUS)

FIRST MAN When the news got around—

SECOND MAN There were many in Leucadia who couldn't quite bring themselves to believe the enormity of it.

FIRST WOMAN   Shock gave way to anger.

SECOND WOMAN   And revulsion to shame.

THIRD WOMAN   Except for those who said . . .

FIRST MAN   What's the fuss? They're just niggers. A black one and two whites ones. It didn't stop a checker game.

SECOND MAN   Among the Negroes of Leucadia—

THIRD MAN   There was no surprise.

FIRST WOMAN   Merely a blinding of the soul.

FIRST MAN   It was the wish of the parents and wives of Lou Marcus and Jeff Lawton that their bodies be buried on either side of Lloyd Lewis in the Lewis family plot in Leucadia.

SECOND WOMAN   But there wasn't a mortician in the county, black or white, who would agree to handle or transport the bodies.

FIRST MAN   The funerals took place.

FIRST WOMAN   One in Detroit.

SECOND WOMAN   One in Boston.

THIRD WOMAN   And one in Leucadia.

FIRST MAN   And for the first time since the trouble started—

SECOND MAN   Hundreds upon hundreds of Negroes . . .

THIRD MAN From every county of the state and beyond . . .

FIRST MAN Took over the streets of Leucadia, unhindered.

FIRST WOMAN Crowding them from curb to curb.

SECOND WOMAN Mourners, black and white, marched.

THIRD WOMAN Silent, soundless.

FIRST WOMAN Except for the scuff of shoes on the asphalt pavement.

FIRST MAN At the cemetery they found their voices.
(In the background we hear the soft singing of "We Shall Overcome")

FIRST WOMAN The hills echoed with their grief.

SECOND WOMAN The skies with their prayers.

THIRD WOMAN The winds carried their song.
(The words of "We Shall Overcome" are distinct for a moment, then continue in the background)

FIRST MAN And when it was over—

SECOND MAN The crowd dispersed.

FIRST WOMAN Some returning to the church.

SECOND WOMAN Some to the Lewis home.

THIRD WOMAN Others to the bus depot and railroad station.

FIRST MAN   Up a pathway from the cemetery—

FIRST WOMAN   A couple climbed, hand-in-hand, through the deep grass—

SECOND WOMAN   Standing breathless as they reached the hilltop overlooking the town.
   (*The lights have dimmed out with the background music; lights then pick out* JEAN *and* DON *standing on the hilltop*)

JEAN   I'm thinking of Betty in Detroit, and wondering how she's holding up.

DON   As well as any girl who's just buried her husband.

JEAN   I wish they could have been buried together. It would have had more meaning.

DON   Funny how culverts, unlike cemeteries in Leucadia, seem to be color-blind.

JEAN   Crazy town you picked to be born in.

DON   How blind *I* was. I used to go to the movies at the Bijou and it didn't seem strange that the whites sat downstairs and the blacks up. They called it "nigger heaven." Wonder if Lloyd's gone to a nigger heaven.

JEAN   That's a macabre thing to say.

DON   The whole thing's macabre. Why not "separate but equal" heavens and hells?

JEAN   I prefer to think that the hereafter—if there is a hereafter—is a little more sane.

DON I'm not settling for the hereafter. I don't happen to believe in it. Any more than I can accept the idea of death . . . Funny, animals never kill their own—except for man. Is that why we were given minds?

JEAN Ironic, isn't it? Personally, I like life. What there is of it.

DON So do I. That's why I'm angry. Because there's so little.

JEAN There certainly wasn't much for Lou, Lloyd, and Jeff.

DON Look, why don't we get away for a few days, hop a train for Atlanta?

JEAN I can't, Don. I'm committed till the end of August.

DON Just for the weekend. Roger and Sarah will be around. Let's take these few moments together while we still can.

JEAN Why do you say *while we still can?*

DON Because we've just come from a funeral and a lot may happen before the end of August.

JEAN (*Turning to him*) Why don't you level with me, Don?

DON I just did.

JEAN No. You've got something on your mind that you're not telling me. (DON *is silent*) What is it? Damn it! Don't be so long-suffering and noble. I *know* there's something. I've known for a long time. Please, I'm worried.

DON (*Takes a few steps, and turns*) All right, you asked for it . . . I saw everything that happened. I was there. I saw it all, Jean. The whole thing from beginning to end.

JEAN (*Pulling in her breath*) Oh, God . . . Have you told anyone?

DON I made that anonymous phone call to Stanley Reeves.

JEAN Otherwise?

DON Otherwise not a soul. I should have. I should have gone to Reeves or the FBI and reported it the night it happened.

JEAN I wish you'd told me.

DON I couldn't. You know why? Because I was ashamed to admit that I'd just stood by and watched.

JEAN There wasn't anything else you could do.

DON I could have yelled. I could have thrown myself at them. Lou and Jeff did.

JEAN And you'd have been killed as they were.

DON That was my rationalization. There had to be an eyewitness.

JEAN It's true, isn't it?

DON Have you seen me running to tell? Heard me shouting it from the roofs?

JEAN The discovery of those three bodies has had more impact than all the lynchings since the Civil War.

DON It was a weasel way of doing it. The story hasn't been told. Not one gory tenth of it.

JEAN It'll come out—sooner or later.

DON I've always known how it'd end. That's what makes me so goddamn furious! You must think a lot of me.

JEAN For being human and honest? You could have left town the next morning.

DON Don't think I didn't want to.

JEAN But you stayed. Stop beating yourself, Don. It isn't simple.

DON It's as simple as having the guts to do it.

JEAN (*Emotionally*) You think I'm not scared? I've been trembling ever since you told me! I'm not urging you to do it. I'm shaking . . .

DON I shouldn't have told you.

JEAN Yes. You should. You've got to have someone you can talk to.

DON Actually, the reason I've been pushing for the Atlanta trip is that I wanted us to have those few days together before I went in to tell Reeves.

JEAN We still can.

DON Would you?

JEAN I want to. Yes.
(*They kiss, clinging together in a long embrace*)

DON (*As they break from their embrace*) As a matter of fact, I think I'd rather go in now. Get it over with. Otherwise it'll be with us every second.

JEAN Are you sure you want to?

DON I don't. I want to chop it out of my stupid brain. I want to shanghai you off to the Aegean Isles and never return. But it isn't as though I ever really had a choice. I'd better go.

JEAN (*With a sudden cry*) No! Not yet. Not for a minute. (*She throws her arms around him, and holds him against her*)

DON Maybe we'll go when it's over. Would you like that?

JEAN (*In a small voice*) Yes.

DON (*Breaking from their embrace*) We'd better start down before I weaken and change my mind.
     (*They start off, arms around each other, as the lights dim. In the darkness a voice is heard*)

VOICE OF REDEEMER SHORTWAVE R-D-1 reporting. R-D-1 reporting. Tindall boy spotted in car with COFO girl. Followed car to COFO Center, where he dropped girl. Followed him up Elm to Briggs building. He has just parked car. Is entering building. Yes, I might have guessed —like seeks like—Mistuh Don (white nigger) Tindall has just entered the offices of Mistuh Stanley (white nigger) Reeves. Interesting . . . I wonder why?
     (*Lights go up on* STANLEY REEVES *seated behind the desk,* DON *seated facing him, with his secretary at the stenotype*)

93

DON   Man's a pretty violent creature. We know it, but seeing it is something else again. Compared to what that hooded mob did to Lloyd Lewis, the crucifixion was an act of mercy. I saw them take off their ridiculous costumes, saw their faces—and their souls, nakedly exposed. It wasn't pretty.

REEVES   Do you remember who they were?

DON   I'll remember them to my grave, starting with Supreme Wizard Dorrance R. Medford and continuing . . .
   (*As the lights dim on* REEVES' *office, lights come up on the* SHERIFF's *office.* DON's *voice continues, but it is now a mechanical voice on tape listened to by* SHERIFF PLUNKETT, DEPUTY SHERIFF ALLEN, DORRANCE MEDFORD, ROY BREWSTER, *and* STEVE CALLOWAY)

DON's VOICE   Our esteemed Sheriff Amos Plunkett, Deputy Sheriff Clyde Allen, Roy Brewster, Steve Calloway, Al Burroughs, Ben Clark, Al Wilson—

SHERIFF   All right, take it into the other room. We've got work to do.
   (*The mechanism is removed, though* DON's *voice is still heard, blurred and indistinct in the background*)

STEVE   That friggin', nigger-lovin' rat! That dirty—

SHERIFF   Save it. The question is how do we handle it?

DEPUTY SHERIFF ALLEN   He's not going to appear as any witness, that's a cinch.

DORRANCE MEDFORD   He's going to meet with an accident.

94

DEPUTY SHERIFF ALLEN A fatal accident.

STEVE Like a bullet through his head.

SHERIFF No. We don't want any of that.

ROY The hell we don't!

SHERIFF We just want to get him in and sign a paper re-
pudiatin' that false statement he just made. Clyde, you just
hop over there and pick him up the minute he comes out
of Reeves' office.

DEPUTY SHERIFF ALLEN For what?

SHERIFF Questioning.

DEPUTY SHERIFF ALLEN On what charge?

SHERIFF Violation of state law 109. (DEPUTY SHERIFF
ALLEN *starts out*) And I don't want him roughed up, understand? We're just goin' to sit down and talk sense with
him.
    (ALLEN *exits*)

DORRANCE MEDFORD You're not going to talk him into
signing any repudiation.

SHERIFF Suppose you leave that to me.

DORRANCE MEDFORD You better have a good excuse for
holdin' him. That bastard Reeves is goin' to use all the
power of the Justice Department to try to spring him.

SHERIFF The Justice Department has no jurisdiction over
state law 109.

95

STEVE What in hell's state law 109?

SHERIFF A statute prohibitin' the solicitation by one male of another to engage in improper and indecent—

STEVE Hell, he's no queer. Why, he and—

SHERIFF Know any better reason why he changed his mind about marryin' Gwen?

STEVE Who'd he solicit?

SHERIFF Roy here.

ROY You kiddin'?

SHERIFF Hell no. You came in and reported it.

ROY I did?

SHERIFF Why, you just got through tellin' me. You were takin' a leak in the Forrest Park men's room. Don Tindall come in, stepped up to the urinal next to yours.

ROY I told you that?

SHERIFF Course you did. And then he turned to you and made an indecent proposal.

ROY What was that?

SHERIFF Shoot, man. He invited you up to his house and said he'd pleasure you by gratifyin' your member. Now weren't those his words?

ROY I guess so.

SHERIFF You don't guess. You assert with indignation! You make charges! Is that clear?

ROY Yeah, I guess.

SHERIFF Forget the guesses. I asked you whether that's exactly what you recalled he said.

ROY Exactly. And I recall I told him to take off or I'd cut his off.

SHERIFF It's comin' back to you now, is it?

ROY Yeah, it's comin' back clear.

DORRANCE MEDFORD That COFO girl. You think Tindall told her?

SHERIFF Perhaps. Though we can pretty much discredit anything she has to say.
(*He flicks the lever of the intercom box*)

VOICE OVER INTERCOM Yessir, Sheriff.

SHERIFF Ned. That nigger in twelve. The one in on that knifing charge.

VOICE OVER INTERCOM Emanuel.

SHERIFF Right. Bring him in. (*He flicks the lever back*) That's a mean one. Has three nigger whores workin' for him. Cut one up for holding back four bits . . . All right, let's break it up. I want to talk to this Emanuel boy alone.
(*The others exit. The* SHERIFF *flicks lever on the intercom again*)

VOICE ON INTERCOM   Yes, Sheriff.

SHERIFF   Dick, you're on duty tonight, aren't you?

VOICE   Yessir.

SHERIFF   Well, I've got a special assignment I want to talk to you about. You're going to need your camera. I'll come in and brief you on it in a few minutes. (*He flicks the lever. There is a knock on the door*) Come in, Ned. (NED, *a guard, and* EMANUEL, *a big Negro of about forty, enter*) Sit down, boy. (*He does so*) There's a little favor you can do for me, boy.

EMANUEL   Yassuh.

SHERIFF   You have any feelin' about this trouble-makin' COFO outfit?

EMANUEL   Nosuh.

SHERIFF   And you wouldn't object if I had that knifing charge dropped, now would you?

EMANUEL   Nosuh.

SHERIFF   All right, then, maybe I can arrange it if you'll
. . .

> (*The lights dim out. Lights up on COFO Center. The phone is ringing.* ROGER, *who sits at the desk, picks it up*)

ROGER   Hello. This is he . . . Jason Collins? Yes. When was this? I see . . . All right, I'll be right over. Thank you.

(*He hangs up.* SARAH *and* JEAN, *both in short night-gowns, have come into the scene*)

SARAH   What happened?

ROGER   Jason was in a car accident. That was the County Hospital. I'd better get over there.

SARAH   I'll go with you.

ROGER   No, it's not that serious. You better stay with Jean. That kid brother of mine! I'll be right back.
(*He exits*)

JEAN   Don't worry about us. Don told me he'd be in by eleven—and it's about that now.

SARAH   What was he doin' in a car at this hour? He knows better than that.

JEAN   As long as it isn't serious, Sarah.

SARAH   I suppose . . . (*She sighs*) I'm exhausted. I'm getting back to bed. Good-night.
(*She exits*)

JEAN   Good-night, Sarah.
(*Lights dim. Simultaneously, a spot comes up on* JEAN's *bed. She crosses, gets into bed, props up a pillow, picks up book, and starts reading. After a long moment we hear the sound of a key turning in a lock and a door opening. A figure can be seen moving through the darkness*)

99

JEAN   Don? Is that you, Don?
(EMANUEL *appears in lighted area*)

EMANUEL   Don couldn't make it tonight. He asked me to
come and tell you.

JEAN (*Frightened*)   Who are you? What happened to him?

EMANUEL   Nothin'. I'm a friend. He changed his plans. He
had to leave town.

JEAN (*With growing apprehension*)   How'd you get in?
I've never seen you at the Center before.

EMANUEL   He gimme his key. He didn't want you to be
alone. He want you taken care of. (*He starts unbuttoning
his shirt*) You don't need to be afraid of me. That's what
I'm here for. To take care of you.
(*He pulls off his shirt*)

JEAN (*Starting up out of the bed*)   Sarah!
(SARAH *starts to answer. Her voice is immediately
muffled. A struggle is heard*)

JEAN (*On her feet*)   Get out of here! Get out! Please!
(*She starts to run past him. He seizes hold of her and
clasps her body against his, hiking up her nightgown.
A flash bulb goes off.* JEAN *turns in panic. He still
holds her. Another flash goes off.* DEPUTY SHERIFF
ALLEN *and the photographer are now visible*)

DEPUTY SHERIFF ALLEN   Get into your clothes, both of
you. I'm taking you down for questioning.

JEAN   Questioning about what?

DEPUTY SHERIFF ALLEN   Obvious, isn't it? We have information that this Center is a cover for a bawdy house.

(JEAN *breaks into an incredulous laugh, but the laughter, tinged with hysteria, turns to sobbing. The lights dim. A spot comes up on* DON's *perspiring face; he is seated in a chair. Around him, in a semicircle, we see a group including* SHERIFF PLUNKETT *and* DEPUTY SHERIFF ALLEN. DON *seems near the point of collapse*)

SHERIFF   You admit you were convinced the Redeemers set fire to your house?

DON (*Wearily*)   Yes.

SHERIFF   But you don't know for a fact that they did? You have no evidence?

DON   No.

SHERIFF   You figured they did, based on the fact that you were associatin' with that COFO crowd, and knew they knew it and didn't approve. Is that right?

DON   Yes.

SHERIFF   Now, would you, without evidence, charge them before a court with settin' fire to your house?

DON   No.

SHERIFF   Yet you did make a flat statement namin' names and accusin' the Redeemers of killin' the three boys.

DON   We've been over that a thousand times. And nothing you say or do is—

SHERIFF   What am I doin' to you, Tindall? Not a thing but sit here and reason with you.

DON   I'm not signing any letter of retraction.

SHERIFF   Is anyone forcin' you to? . . . We've had enough trouble in this town. The world's lookin' at us, Tindall. Can't I make you see that your statement, comin' on top of the discovery of those bodies, is going to split things wide open?
(*He gets up, comes around the desk*)

DON   Maybe they should be.

SHERIFF   (*Sitting on the desk, facing* DON) Look, Don. Both of us were born and raised in this town. And what's happened is a tragic thing. It can ruin everything we've built up here. Businesses, honor, reputations.

DON   It's a little late to think of that now, Sheriff.

SHERIFF   I'm pleading with you to think of the consequences, not for the guilty but for the innocent, the hundreds of men who'll be thrown out of work, their wives and children. Let this thing lie, Tindall. Give the town a chance.

DON   The only chance it has is to face up to what's happened. You're supposed to *uphold* the law, Sheriff.

SHERIFF   (*Walking away*) When'd you ever see me break it?

DON   The statement tells when.

SHERIFF (*Turning*) You didn't see me. Because I wasn't there. And neither were you.

DON My statement stands.

SHERIFF Your statement's a fabrication. A lie. Just as all your stories are lies. I went to grade school with you, Tindall. I remember the stories you used to tell. You'd sit in that cabin smokin' cornsilk with your nigger buddy Lloyd, and come back with tales about hearin' drums and seein' voodoo spirits rise from the swamp, and dance and prance around.
(DEPUTY SHERIFF ALLEN *chuckles*)

DON I made up stories as a kid. What of it?

SHERIFF In Miss Kelsey's class you said you could believe Joan of Arc heard voices and saw visions because you did, too. Are you sure your story of the killings wasn't based on some such vision?

DON It was no vision.

SHERIFF I can produce fifty people who can tell about stories you insisted were real.

DON This isn't a story! It's a fact.

SHERIFF I don't think for one minute that you can tell fact from fiction. You're what is known as a congenital liar, Tindall. Do you think a jury's goin' to believe you?

DON A jury from this county or state may not, but the world will.

SHERIFF   Isn't that why you started makin' up your stories, Tindall? Because you wanted attention? Isn't that what you're after now?

DON   (*His voice rising*)   I want attention for what happened, yes.

SHERIFF   You're bein' very foolish, Tindall. You don't think anyone's goin' to take the word of a proven pervert?

DON   (*Rising*)   You can't prove that stupid homosexual charge and you know it!

SHERIFF   Very foolish, considering there are witnesses who will—

DON   Roy Brewster's word—

SHERIFF   Is as good as that of a nigger-lovin' pervert's. Better.

DEPUTY SHERIFF ALLEN   You didn't go to that cabin in the woods with your nigger-buddy Lloyd just to smoke corn-silk.

DON   (*Wheeling on him*)   You bastard! Don't you imply that Lloyd and I—

DEPUTY SHERIFF ALLEN   I'm not implyin'. I know.
(*He shoves* DON *back into the chair*)

SHERIFF   I can put at least three of your classmates on the stand who observed you in acts of buggery in that cabin.

DON   That's a vicious lie! And if you had any respect for the dead—

SHERIFF   Did you have any respect for the dead when, on the night of your folks' funeral, you had that nigger over to their house and engaged in similar acts?

DON *(Jumps up and swings at* SHERIFF, *who ducks)*   You sonofabitch! You warped, filthy-minded sonofabitch!
     *(*DEPUTY SHERIFF ALLEN *catches his arms from behind and slams him back into the chair)*

SHERIFF   All right now, cool it. You sit there till you cool off . . . Get him some water, Clyde . . . *(*DEPUTY SHERIFF ALLEN *exits)* You don't seem to realize that when you insist on stickin' to that statement, you're in for a—

DON   You've made it quite clear, what I'm in for.

SHERIFF   You called me a sonofabitch. Well, I can *be* a sonofabitch. I can also be the most generous man in the world. Withdraw that statement and in five seconds you'll be out of here, free and clear and with all charges dropped and expunged from the record. *(*DEPUTY SHERIFF ALLEN *returns and hands the* SHERIFF *a cup of water)* Here, you sip on it and consider whether that isn't the smartest thing you can do. Play ball with me and—

DON   I'm not making any bargains, Sheriff!
     (The SHERIFF, *who still holds the cup in his hands, dashes the water in* DON's *face)*

SHERIFF   I'm warning you. I'm losin' my patience. Now you listen to me, Tindall. Your life isn't worth two cents unless you make a retraction. You know that, don't you?

DON   I know you can do to me what you did to them, yes. But I don't think you will. It wouldn't be very smart, considering that Reeves has the statement.

SHERIFF It isn't me. You're safe as long as you're in here. It's when you get out.

DON I think it's a little too raw, even for the Redeemers.

SHERIFF Folks don't like the idea of anyone gettin' up on the stand and accusin' 'em of murder.

DON Whether I'm dead or alive the statement still will. And Reeves isn't the only one I told what happened.

SHERIFF You talkin' about that COFO whore?

DON Don't you call her that.

SHERIFF Give it to me, Clyde. (CLYDE *hands him a photo, which the* SHERIFF *in turn hands to* DON) You think anyone's goin' to believe a girl who's been layin' for niggers in that cathouse you call a community center?

DON (*Ripping photo*) You dirt! You scum! You sick, twisted—
    (*He starts to leap at the* SHERIFF, *but the* SHERIFF *anticipates him and hits him with a blow to the stomach that sends him staggering to the floor. He doubles up with a groan of agony*)

SHERIFF You been askin' for it and now you're goin' to get it! Put the cuffs on him. (*Cuffs are snapped on* DON's *wrists*) All right, Tindall. This is your last chance. One way or another you're going to end up withdrawing that statement. Now, do you want to do it unwillingly, or do you want to be persuaded?

DON (*In agonized voice*) I'm not going to withdraw it.

SHERIFF   All right, he wants to be persuaded. He's all yours, Clyde.

DEPUTY SHERIFF ALLEN   Okay, Tindall. Up. Up on your feet . . .
(*He yanks* DON *up by the handcuffs*)

SHERIFF   I'm going to have me a nap. If he appears to want to change his mind, wake me.
(*He puts his feet on the desk and leans back in the chair*)

DEPUTY SHERIFF ALLEN (*Starts toward* DON *as lights begin to dim*)   All right, 'Tindall. I've been waiting for this. (*The lights dim out as he shoves* DON *toward the exit. In the darkness the sound of a fist crashing against a jaw can be heard. Lights up on the* SHER-IFF's *office. The* SHERIFF *is at the desk,* MEDFORD *is pacing, and* STEVE GRAYSON *is in the chair*)

MEDFORD   The sonofabitch is tougher than I thought he was.

STEVE   I don't get it. What the hell's he holding out for? Does he think anyone's going to be convicted?

SHERIFF   No. He knows the score.

STEVE   Then what?

MEDFORD   He's one of those damn-fool idealists who believe in justice—justice for the nigger.

SHERIFF   I don't agree with his thinkin'. But you wanna know somethin'? I admire him. I admire his guts.

MEDFORD   You goin' soft on us, Sheriff?

SHERIFF   No. I can't afford to. Once you start down this road there's no turnin' back. But if I had it to do over again, I don't know that I'd go the same way.

MEDFORD   The only other way is to give in to 'em.

SHERIFF   I thought I had it all figured out. You stop something dead, or you let it get out of hand. Sacrifice a few to avoid a lot more ruckus and killing later. It worked before. It doesn't seem to be now.

MEDFORD   You don't know that.

SHERIFF   There comes a time when you've got to realize you're licked. We were licked a hundred years ago—they thought! But we didn't act it. We called the tune and everyone danced to it. Well, I'm beginning to think it's caught up with us. I'm not so sure we didn't make a mistake with those boys. (*The sound of a blow and* DON's *cry are heard*) I don't like that. I don't like it at all.

STEVE   I wish the hell you'd give me a crack at him. I'd break him down or else.

SHERIFF   It's the "or else" we don't want. We need a signature, not a corpse.

MEDFORD   He holds out long enough and that's what you'll get.
(*The* SHERIFF *flips the intercom's lever*)

VOICE OVER INTERCOM   Yes, Sheriff.

SHERIFF Clyde, take a break. All of you. I'm sendin' out for coffee and—

DEPUTY SHERIFF ALLEN We could use some.

SHERIFF Tell Tindall he can have some, too, if he signs his name. You hear me, Tindall? What do you say?

DEPUTY SHERIFF ALLEN He hears, but he's not sayin'.

SHERIFF All right, let him lay there a while. I think he's had enough to realize he doesn't want any more. Just let him ponder it. Because I'm tellin' you this, Tindall. We can go a lot longer than you can. For God's sake, man, use your head!
    (*He flips the lever. The lights dim out. A low-keyed overhead spot throws a cone of light on* DON, *who lies on the floor, his face on his arms.* DON's *and* JEAN's *speeches in this sequence are soliloquies, and though their thoughts seem to be addressed to each other, they face away from each other*)

DON (*His voice is hoarse and weak*) Jean . . . They're killing me, Jean . . . My name. All I have to do is sign my name. Should I, Jean?

JEAN (*Spot on* JEAN *on the other side of the stage*) What're they doing to you, Don? I keep thinking of what they did to the boys and I can't help— Oh, God, why do I keep coming back to it? Maybe Reeves can get you out in the morning. If the morning isn't too late. If they haven't already— *No, they can't! They don't dare!*

DON Why'd I have to spoil things? I should have known. They bugged the Center. Why not his office?

JEAN I wanted to say, "Don't, Don! Let it wait." But I let you go. It's the right thing to do, I told myself. Was it?

DON We're such innocents, Jean . . . such innocents.

JEAN Why'd I let my sense of right play into the hands of evil? This didn't have to happen! Why did I let it? Why, Don? Why did I fail you?

DON My name . . . So easy . . . Do you know something? I never even saw you dance.

JEAN We never really got to know each other.

DON When I was ten, I used to go to Miss Manning's class in social dancing. It was all so proper and genteel. We always ended with a waltz. May I have the pleasure of the next dance, Miss Portugal?

JEAN You may, indeed.
(*The shafts of light from the spots on* DON *and* JEAN *leave them and move downstage, pausing as they reach each other. An old recording of "It's Three O'Clock in the Morning" is heard. The shafts of light, as if holding on two dancers, move around to the waltz rhythm*)

DON'S VOICE You *are* a good dancer, Miss Portugal.

JEAN'S VOICE It's so easy to follow your lead, Mr. Tindall.

DON'S VOICE Waltzes aren't in fashion any more.

JEAN'S VOICE But I love them . . . I always have . . .
(*The two shafts of light continue to move to the music for a few bars. The music fades, the shafts of*

light dance offstage. A sharp oblong of light from the wings hits DON's *still, prone body. We see the boots of the* SHERIFF *and* DEPUTY SHERIFF *step into the light)*

SHERIFF   Well, Tindall, what's the verdict? Have you decided to be sensible? (*Silence*) What about it, Tindall? Are you going to sign that paper?

DON (*After another pause, his voice weary*)   No.

SHERIFF (*Wearily*)   All right, Clyde, he still wants to be persuaded.
          (*Two figures step into the light, then bend down and grab hold of* DON. *The light blacks out. Sounds of blows and* DON's *reaction to them are heard. Lights come up on the* CHORUS OF COMMENTATORS)

FIRST MAN   For three hours exactly . . .

SECOND MAN   With measured intervals out for reflection . . .

THIRD MAN   The process of *persuasion* continued.

FIRST WOMAN   Thirty seconds later, it was over.

SECOND WOMAN   He had passed out twice before, and each time had been revived.

THIRD WOMAN   Not this time.

FIRST WOMAN   Not water.

SECOND WOMAN   Or mouth-to-mouth resuscitation.

FIRST MAN   Not a pulmotor.

SECOND MAN   Or an incision and hand massage.

THIRD MAN   Could bring the beat back to his heart.

FIRST MAN   The Sheriff, like an old songsmith unable to let go of a stubborn tune—

SECOND MAN   Played it through to the end.

THIRD MAN   The unfortunate tragedy, he stated, was the result of a homosexual assault by Tindall on the prisoner who shared his cell. The prisoner, in self-defense, struck him a wild blow which sent him crashing against the concrete wall. His right temple got the full force of the impact, and he fell to the floor. By the time the guard was summoned, Tindall was dead.

FIRST MAN   A witness from the opposite cell.

SECOND MAN   Confirmed the story.

THIRD MAN   The pathologist's report corroborated it.

FIRST MAN   "Death by accidental blow," read the coroner's finding.

FIRST WOMAN   There were some who questioned.

SECOND WOMAN   Some who found the story inconsistent with the man they knew.

THIRD MAN   The great majority—

THIRD WOMAN   Quick to seize on the sins of others to mitigate their own—

FIRST MAN   Accepted it as true.

FIRST WOMAN   He always was a little on the effeminate side.

SECOND WOMAN   Did you ever notice the way he used his wrists?

SECOND MAN   Hell, he couldn't throw a baseball overhand.

FIRST MAN   For "jurisdictional reasons," the case never came to trial.

FIRST WOMAN   But there *was* an indictment.

SECOND WOMAN   The statement was introduced.

FIRST MAN   It was reported in the press.

SECOND MAN   Ironically—

THIRD MAN   It was substantiated by a member of the White Redeemers.

FIRST MAN   Who, for a reward of twenty-five thousand . . .

SECOND MAN   Turned in his brothers.

THIRD MAN   And spilled his guts.

FIRST WOMAN   On a quiet Sunday, three days after his death . . .

SECOND WOMAN   Don Tindall was buried.
(*Lights come up on* ROGER, *who stands on a stair. The* CHORUS *breaks into the crowd around him*)

ROGER This is the fifth time this year that I speak at a funeral that should not be. The fifth time—and it's five times too many. I'm tired of coming to such funerals, tired of the untimely farewells, tired of groping for nonexistent words to give solace when there is no solace. There is no substitute for life, for a smile, a look of love. Weep, Jean. Yes, weep, Betty, Shirley, and Anne. Weep for the youth and goodness so suddenly and savagely removed. I'm tired, sick and tired of looking down into coffins cradling maimed bodies that once were men. I'm tired, perhaps too tired. Perhaps there is more hope than I think. For Don Tindall was no hot-eyed rebel. He was a white Southerner, reluctant as any to get involved, and he didn't have to. Didn't have to follow and see what he saw, didn't have to risk his life to tell it. But he wanted the world to know. And whether the murderers are caught and tried and punished, the world *does* know! It knows the who, what, and how of this monstrous deed, which this town can never eradicate or expiate. That is his victory, even though his killers live and he is dead. I salute him for it, and I say, damn them! Damn them to hell for what they've done! (*His voice breaks*) I don't want ever again to come to another of these funerals. Enough! Isn't it time we had enough!

   (*Lights dim on* ROGER *and simultaneously come up on the* CHORUS, *which quickly gets into formation*)

FIRST MAN Three years have gone by.

SECOND MAN A civil rights and voting law have been enacted.

THIRD MAN And many, who couldn't before, have now registered.

FIRST WOMAN   Surprisingly, the world hasn't come to an end.

SECOND WOMAN   Nor has it really changed.

FIRST MAN   True, signs reading "Colored" and "White" have been removed.

THIRD WOMAN   Twenty-three Negro girls and boys now attend white schools so that Leucadia qualifies for Federal funds.

SECOND MAN   And the Green Lantern Restaurant will even find a table for an occasional Negro customer.

FIRST MAN   But the Redeemers still meet in the hills.

SECOND MAN   A black man walking down the highway may still be ambushed and peppered with shot.

THIRD MAN   And a white sports car can suddenly plough into a crowd of Negro marchers at forty miles an hour, then swerve away, with a white girl's voice screaming—

FIRST WOMAN   You black nigger bastards, I wouldn't dirty my car on you!

SECOND WOMAN   No, the millennium hasn't come.

FIRST MAN   Still, in a state flying a Confederate flag . . .

SECOND WOMAN   A black sheriff was elected.

THIRD MAN   Twenty Negroes, for the first time this century, sit in Southern legislatures.

FIRST MAN   And a white sheriff who wore a button proclaiming "Never!"

SECOND MAN   Removed it to court the black vote.

SECOND WOMAN   And lost.

FIRST MAN   It isn't "Now."

SECOND MAN (*Quietly*)   But neither is it "Never!"
(*Lights dim out on the* CHORUS. *Simultaneously a spotlight comes up on* JEAN)

JEAN   Leucadia would like, if it could, to forget Lou, Lloyd, Jeff, and Don. It cannot. Before he left the office of Stanley Reeves, Don dictated a will. From the ashes of the old Tindall house, a phoenix *has* finally risen. The acreage has been turned into a park. In it stands an auditorium which is their monument. It demands attention. So does the bronze relief of their faces. In a large studio, I rehearse with my girls, who become increasingly expert. Last night we gave a recital. It was open to the public, and two hundred were in the audience. It wasn't anything spectacular. One of the numbers was enlarged from the improvisation the girls were working on the first time Don came to the Center, "The Earth, the Sky, and People All Around." (*Softly, in the background, a reprise of the piano accompaniment used for the improvisation is heard*) What, you are probably asking, could be less important than a modern dance recital, by amateurs, in Godforsaken Leucadia? I don't know, really. But there was something terribly moving about it. Perhaps because the girls looked so lovely in their costumes, perhaps because they were so eager and happy and dignified. Perhaps because the audi-

ence was so appreciative and proud. I know I was. And I
think Don would have been, too.

*(The music continues for a moment as the lights
fade)*

Curtain